Staten Island

The Other Cradle of
Aviation

By

Ed Drury

Icarus Aviation Press

Columbia, Iowa

Text Copyright 2011 Ed Drury

Cover designed by Jen Elia (EliaJenn@aol.com)

All Rights Reserved.
No part of this publication mey be reproduced, stored in a retrieval system, or transmitted in any form by any electronic or mechanical copying system without the written permission of the publisher.

Printed in U.S.A.

987654321

First Edition

ISBN: 978-0-9724527-2-4

Published by:
Icarus Aviation Press
2459 Highway 14
Columbia, IA 50057
USA
www.icarusbooks.com

Contents

Acknowledgments.. 5

Chapter 1... 7
   The Early Years

Chapter 2... 11
   Charles R. Wittemann

Chapter 3... 25
   Richmond County Fair

Chapter 4... 29
   Confusion - Baldwin, Baldwin, White Wing, Red Wing, Red Devil, and Ailerons

Chapter 5... 33
   Oakwood Heights Airport

Chapter 6... 37
   George N. Boyd

Chapter 7... 41
   Ted Lovington

Chapter 8... 45
   The Unsolved Mystery of Bert Jewell

Chapter 9... 49
   Miller Field

Chapter 10 57
   Giuseppe Mario Bellanca

Chapter 11 65
   George G. Fernic

Chapter 12 ... 73
Fox Hills Golf Course

Chapter 13 ... 75
Donovan-Hughes Airport

Chapter 14 ... 83
Staten Island Airport

Chapter 15 ... 89
Richmond County Airport

Chapter 16 ... 93
Aviation Locations on Staten Island

Chapter 17 ... 97
Time Line

Chapter 18 ... 101
Staten Island Aviators and Enthusiasts

Chapter 19 ... 107
Specifications of Some Aircraft Mentioned in This Book

Chapter 20 ... 113
Bellanca Aircraft Records and Accolades

Appendix ... 115
C. & A. Wittemann Catalog

Photo Credits... ... 141

Acknowledgments

The author would like to express his sincere thanks to the following individuals and organizations for their help in making this book possible:

Glen Adamo
Tom Andrews
Walter Boyne
Francis Cardamone
Felice Ciccione
Dan Cullman
Burt Davis
Marie DeClerico
Tom Dee
Kari Dienstadt
John DiForte
Ed Fanuzzi
George Frebert
Emma Gallop
Louis Judice
Jack Lorino
Ted Lovington
Mrs. Emily Miller
Charles Modzelewski
Tom Moore
Doug Morgan
Mark Nathans
John Olson
Andy Origlia
Steve Remington
Bette Johnson Sohrn
Jim Stamper
Elinor Smith Sullivan
August Tornquist

Aerofiles.com
Aviation Hall of Fame & Museum of New Jersey, Teterboro, NJ
Gateway National Recreation Area

National Air & Space Museum, Smithsonian Institution, Washington, DC
New England Air Museum, Windsor Locks, CT
Staten Island Historical Society
Staten Island Museum of Arts and Sciences

Chapter 1

The Early Years - The Turn of the 20th Century

The year was 1907, on a field in Little Clove Valley on Staten Island the first powered, commercially produced airplane in the United States took to the air. There was very little fanfare. Some local farmers and a few onlookers witnessed the event. The significance of this flight has been lost to history.

While this was the beginning of powered flight on Staten Island, it was by no means the beginning of aviation for the Island.

Long before Staten Islanders heard the roar of airplane engines over their island, the Staten Island Flying Club was already having meetings. I first found reference to this club in the Richmond County Democrat, printed December 19, 1896.

> **S. I. Flying Club.**
>
> The second annual meeting of the S. I. Flying club was held on Tuesday evening, at VanDam's hall, New Brighton. The following board of directors was unanimously re-elected: J. H. Thompson, president; A. Doyle and A. Sohm, vice-presidents; James Hughes, treasurer and Chas. Bang, secretary.

From the Richmond County Democrat, December 19, 1896.

The newspaper reported the meeting of this club as the "second annual" meeting, so the club was formed in 1895.

Since this was before powered airplane flight, it can be assumed that the club was formed for ballooning or possibly gliding, as the first successful glider was built in 1891.

The directors mentioned in the article were:
President: J. H. Thompson
Vice Presidents: A. Doyle
                         A. Sohm

Treasurer: James Hughes
Secretary: Charles Bang

This meeting was held at Van Dam's Hall in the New Brighton section of Staten Island. The building that housed Van Dam's Hall is long gone, replaced by stores that are, themselves, now abandoned.

The island was rolling hills, along with many meadows, valleys and plains. This great, once open space is now shopping centers, condos and general urban sprawl.

Otto Lilienthal

With names like New Dorp Plain, Pleasant Valley, Little Clove Valley and Pleasant Plains, it's easy to see why aviation could sprout here.

William Randolph Hearst, of publishing fame, flew on Staten Island before the turn of the century. Mr. Hearst purchased and flew a glider that was built by Otto Lilienthal. Lilienthal, a German engineer, built the most successful gliders of the non-powered flight era. He is considered the first man to fly in controlled, heavier-than-air flight.

Lilienthal died in 1896, in a crash while flying one of his own machines. He, along with Octave Chanute, ushered in the beginning of manned heavier-than-air flight.

One of Lilienthal's gliders, in fact the one flown by Hearst, survives today. It was built in 1884 and it is on display in the Smithsonian's National Air and Space Museum.

Hearst is said to have flown this glider only once. Members of his family and some of his newspaper staff also tried their hand at it.

The lion's share of these flights were flown by a New Jersey athlete, Harry Bodine, who was hired by Hearst as a demonstration pilot. When Lilienthal died in August of 1896, Hearst forbade further flights.

While most of these flights were on his estate on Long Island,

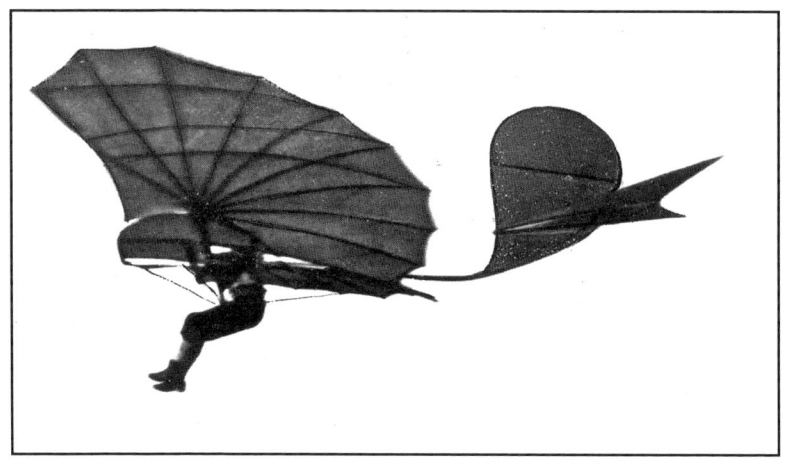

Lilienthal glider.

some of them were flown on Staten Island.

The Wittemann family, including brothers Charles, Adolph, Harold, Paul, Walter and their sister Marie, flew kites prior to 1900, including a man-carrying kite that several of the brothers used for their first flying experience.

In his journal of 1896 Charles Wittemann writes of holding a very large box kite with his feet firmly planted on the ground. However, nature had other ideas. A gust of wind took the kite and young

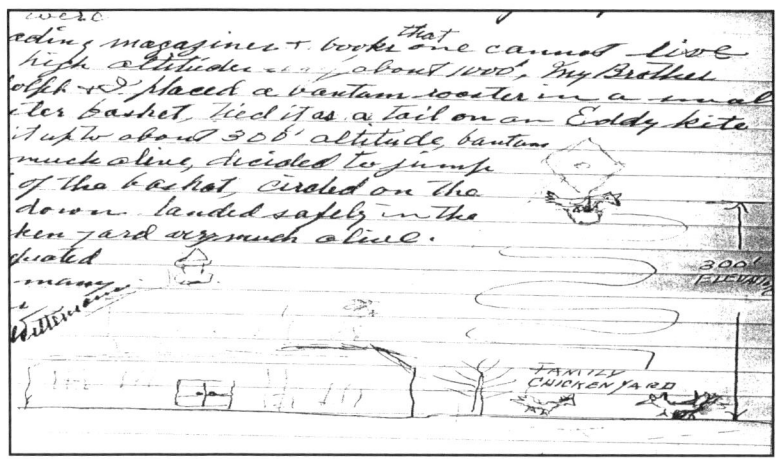

Wittemann's hand drawn sketch.

Charles for a ride. On that day he experienced flight for the first time and he was hooked for life.

In 1895 it was commonly believed that terrestrial animals couldn't survive above 1000 feet. Charles Wittemann decided to prove or disprove this theory. He and his brother Adolph placed a bantam rooster in a basket that was then attached to an "Eddy" kite and, in this manner, they managed to get the rooster to 300 feet. The rooster didn't like this very much and jumped out. He spiraled down and landed in the family hen yard, none the worse for wear. Mr. Wittemann recorded this event in his own hand and even added a hand drawn sketch.

Inspired by news of the Wright Brother's success, small gliding clubs sprung up all over the island.

Chapter 2

Charles R. Wittemann

One of the great pioneers of "heavier than air" aviation, albeit unsung, was Charles R. Wittemann. Mr. Wittemann, along with his previously mentioned brothers, Harold, Paul, Adolph and Walter, built man-carrying kites prior to 1900 and gliders as early as 1900. They manufactured and flew powered aircraft by 1907.

Charles R. Wittemann - 1964

Charles was born in New York City in 1884 and moved to Staten Island with his family in 1885. At the age of 10, whenever time allowed, he was already flying kites. He flew box kites and experimented with carrying weights on board them.

During this period he, for the first time, tried to learn the effects of altitude on living things. He used kites to carry cats and, as stated before, a bantam rooster. He found there to be no ill effects.

In the year of 1896, he was experimenting with very large kites that often required a winch to control. During one of these flights, quite by accident, young Charles went airborne. He was stopped by a tree and managed to tie the kite rope to the tree. That brief flight filled him with awe and the ambition to fly.

In 1900 he built a shop/laboratory near the foot of Ocean Terrace on his father's estate near the center of Staten Island. After careful study of that kite, and it's action in flight, he decided that a kite

The second, and larger, Wittemann factory on Ocean Terrace.

could indeed become a heavier than air, man carrying, flying machine. Mr. Wittemann experimented with single wing designs but finally settled on the biplane configuration. This vast rolling estate had once been home to the Staten Island Vanderbilts. It was built by shipping magnate Commodore Cornelius Vanderbilt for his daughter.

By 1903 Wittemann had a good flying biplane glider. The flight of the Wright brothers gave him the confidence to stay with the biplane design. In 1905, after much improvement, he had designed a very successful glider. This was the model he was to offer for sale. This was the year that he began to build his first factory made machine.

During this glider development period, from 1900 until 1904, Charles Wittemann took employment in a machinery plant (The Pioneer Iron Works, in Brooklyn, NY) where he became a master mechanic. He also attended night classes at Pratt Institute, where he graduated with a degree in mechanical engineering.

To gain experience, in early 1906 Charles took a job as a marine engineer on the Steam Ship St. Louis of the American Line. Upon his return to the U. S. in September of 1906 he began to build and sell gliders in earnest. He also advertised to build airplanes for others. At this time he was operating what was to be the first airplane

"Model II Glider in Towed Flight (1907)."

manufacturing factory in the United States. The first Wittemann designed airplane flew in 1907, a pusher type that was loosely patterned after the Wright Flyer. To assemble this airplane and to supply the aircraft that were by now on order he joined with his brother Adolph and renamed the company C & A Wittemann. The British American Motor Company of Bridgeport, CT manufactured the engine used in this first airplane. The brothers completely disassembled this power plant and modified it by cutting much of the excess metal from it. Whitehead engines powered the next two aircraft and later, Hall-Scott engines were used in Wittemann aircraft. Some of his later airplanes were, at the customer's request, powered by Gnome, Anzani, and Eldridge engines.

Charles Wittemann soloed in 1906 and was a member of the Early Birds of Aviation.

"A Section of Our Factory, Showing Assembling Division."

13

Wittemann built over 200 gliders and about 35 airplanes in his Staten Island factories. His own design was the first powered aircraft from this facility. The first aircraft designed by Wittemann also had the first ailerons ever mounted on an airplane. The Wright brothers and other early pioneers used wing warping. Ailerons became the standard of the industry and are on virtually every powered aircraft in the world today.

The first powered Wittemann aircraft.

In the first decade of the century he even powered a helicopter. Lee S. Burridge, who was, at that time, the president of the Aeronautical Society of America tried to have Gustave Whitehead power this craft with one of his proven engines. After Whitehead refused, correctly claiming that the aircraft could never fly, Burridge turned to Wittemann who had been buying Whitehead engines to power his own aircraft. Wittemann did power the craft but as Whitehead predicted, the helicopter never flew.

This was the same Gustave Whitehead who claimed to fly an airplane two years before the Wright brothers. There are even some newspaper articles to document this.

Wittemann's factory was rolling out powered airplanes in 1907. In contrast, the Wright Brothers didn't build their first commercial airplane until 1908, and Glen Curtiss didn't open his factory doors until 1909.

Baldwin "Red Devil".

In France, Gabriel Voison also opened a factory in 1905. No one knows for sure if this or the Wittemann plant was the first in the world.

The famous Farman airplanes were built in the Voison factory during the same time period as early Wittemann aircraft were being manufactured.

Perhaps the most famous of the Wittemann aircraft were those built with and for Captain Thomas S. Baldwin. The airplane was known as the Baldwin "Red Devil". One of the six or more "Red Devils" that were built resides in the Smithsonian's National Air & Space Museum. This is the only Wittemann-built aircraft known to survive. The Smithsonian purchased it in 1950 from the Roosevelt Field Museum collection.

The Wittemann home on Ocean Terrace was an informal meeting place for aviators of the time. The Wittemann family often hosted breakfast gatherings. The guest list would read like a "who's who" of early aviation. Glen Curtiss, Thomas Scott Baldwin, Katharine and Eddie Stinson, Ruth Law, Harriet Quimby and Lt. Thomas

The only surviving "Red Devil" at the Smithsonian's National Air & Space Museum.

E. Selfridge, along with the members of the great aviation associations of the time and many other pioneer aviators would stop by.

Wittemann had his share of "firsts". Along with his aileron innovation, Wittemann is credited with building the first aircraft with a skeleton of steel tubing (a "Red Devil"). This was the first time steel had been used in this fashion. Hall-Scott powered "Red Devils" were sold commercially beginning in 1912.

Credit for the design and construction of the "Red Devils" is claimed by: The Aeronautical Society of America, Thomas Scott Baldwin, and Charles Wittemann.

When I spoke with Charles Wittemann in 1963 he told me that he had designed the aircraft for Baldwin. In his words "The largest early customer was Capt. Thomas S. Baldwin for whom I developed and built the many famous "Red Devils" he used for exhibition." The first one was built in the Society's shop in Long Island and/or Baldwin's own shop in Oakwood Heights Staten Island. Whoever built it, Wittemann's hand was in it.

Exterior of the Wittemann-Lewis Newark, NJ plant.

The first three "Red Devil's" might have been reincarnations of the original one, each being rebuilt from the wreckage of the previous one. At least three later examples were built at the Wittemann factory on Ocean Terrace and Little Clove Road.

Another famous Wittemann customer was E. Lillian Todd, the first woman to design an airplane.

Two of the Wittemann brothers were instrumental in the formation of the Aeronautical Society of America. Although the society's first field and meeting place was a racetrack in Morris Park, NY, many of the charter members were Staten Islanders.

Wittemann-Barling Bomber.

The Brothers, Charles and Paul Wittemann, joined with their friend Samuel C. Lewis in 1914 to form the Witteman-Lewis Aircraft Company at the site of Wittemann's original factory. At some point they dropped the second N from the Wittemann name for the company name, however, Wittemann personally still used the double N.

The plant was eventually moved to Newark, New Jersey, where they developed and built training planes for the government. They

The Red Devil crash which killed William R. Badger, August 15, 1911.

built the first twin-engine, enclosed fuselage, plane with pontoons. It was test flown from Newark Bay. During this period they also built a pilotless plane for the U.S. Navy. It had Carl Norden instruments and was tested successfully. The first one of these aircraft was delivered on February 26, 1919. They were to be the Navy's first flying bomb. The peacetime navy lost interest and the project never reached operational status.

An airport site in Newark Meadows was surveyed in 1914, where Newark Airport sits today. Except in very dry weather the site was too marshy to support even the light aircraft of the time. They built hangars and a factory building there and abandoned the site after a very short period.

In 1917, the company acquired and moved to a 500-acre plot in Hasbrouck Heights in northern New Jersey. This location was later to become Teterboro Airport. During this period Lewis left the company and the name was changed to Wittemann Aircraft Company. President Wilson appointed Charles Wittemann to the Federal Military Aviation Committee that same year.

The factory at Teterboro was completed in 1918. In 1920 the company was awarded a contract for re-designing and rebuilding a fleet of De Havilland DH-4's for the U.S. Post Office. These aircraft were to be operated by the Air Mail Service.

With the size of the new factory Wittemann was able to bid on the construction of what was to be the largest airplane in the world, the Witteman Barling Bomber. Each airplane had six engines. The aircraft flew very well, but was too heavy for the job and couldn't haul the required payload for any distance.

The Wittemann Company operated at Teterboro until 1925 when

the government failed to pay cost overrun charges and the company was forced out of business.

The land and plant were then sold to the Fokker Airplane Company. Charles Wittemann is considered the founder of Teterboro Airport, and was inducted into the Aviation Hall of Fame there.

There are no known fatalities in any Wittemann designed airplane other then the modified Baldwin "Red Devils" that were built by Wittemann. One fatality was a man named Cecil Peoli, an exhibition pilot who died in 1915 in an aircraft said to be his design, but it was actually a modified Baldwin "Red Devil". The other was William R. Badger, who died at an aviation meet in Chicago on August 15, 1911.

Charles Wittemann died in 1967.

The only thing that remains on Staten Island as a reminder of the original Wittemann factory is a small circular street called Wittemann Place, very near the site of the former assembly building. The valley, at that time called Little Clove Valley, was the flying field for this factory. It is now part of Interstate 278, a six lane highway also called the Staten Island Expressway.

Charles Wittemann's memo for a proposed book is reprinted below, courtesy of Mr. Mark Nathans.

(For the sake of historical accuracy we have printed the memo exactly as written, including any grammatical errors.)

AN INFORMAL HISTORY OF EARLY GLIDER AND AIRPLANE EXPERIMENTS AND LATER ACCOMPLISHMENTS OF CHARLES R. WITTEMANN ONE OF THE FIRST PIONEERS IN AIRPLANE DEVELOPMENT, DESIGN AND MANUFACTURE.

"I became interested in aviation long before flying machines could be made to fly and thru continuous experiments became a veteran flyer, pioneer airplane designer and builder and apparently the first commercial airplane manufacturer.

"Born in New York City in 1884 and from a year later raised on Staten Island, New York City.

"At the age of ten I became an enthusiastic kite flyer, which lead to my interest in aviation. By 1896 I was experimenting with and building different kites that lead to the box-kite types, in which I was able to carry some weight successfully.

"As development progressed I decided to test the effect that flying would have on life, so experimented by carrying cats to heights a line would permit for varying lengths of time. Those tests showed no ill effect on any of the cats, beyond, possibly some fright.

"Later that year I built a large box-kite from the designs and arrangements I had developed. It flew exceptionably well and required a strong line that some times had to be controlled from a drum winch. At one time, while sailing this large kite on a windy day I was dragged off my feet before I could fasten the line. A group of trees were ahead so held on to grasp a hold on a tree where I succeeded in tying the line. That brief flight was a thrilling experience that fired me with the ambition to fly.

"After careful study of that kite and its action in flight, I felt that I had conceived the possibility of a heavier-than-air flying machine. The experience convinced me that the air could support considerable weight with the right type kite, so worked on developing a practical form, which later were called, gliders.

"The next experiments were along the line of birds, or the single wing or mono-plane types, these proved difficult to control in flight. At this time learned of some glider experiments flown by Lillienthal and Langley. While only little data on those experiments could be obtained, it encouraged my developments along the mono-plane types, but by 1901 lead me to a bi-plane type with much greater success.

"To have a shop and laboratory, I built a small building in 1900. The advantage of this facility enabled me to progress more practically and by 1903 developed a good flying bi-plane type glider. The flight of the Wright brothers gave me more confidence that the bi-plane type was good and continued improving my designs until by early 1905 I had a very successful glider design.

"During that period from

WITTEMANN-LEWIS AIRCRAFT COMPANY INC.

Aircraft

Manufacturers

Standard and Special Designs

Ocean Terrace and   STATEN ISLAND
Little Clove Road   NEW YORK CITY
Tel. West Brighton 1629

1916 ad from *Aviation* magazine. At this time there were still two 'n's in the name.

1900 on, to gain practical and engineering experience, I took employment in a machinery manufacturing plant, The Pioneer Iron Works, Brooklyn, N.Y., where I learned to become a master mechanic and during the same time attended night sessions at Pratt Institute's course in Mechanical Engineering, until graduation in 1904

"During the summer of 1906 I had an opportunity to gain experience by substituting as a marine engineer for four months on the S.S. St. Louis of the American Line, then one of the fastest passenger ships sailing between New York and Southampton, England. In September with this added experience I returned to my laboratory to proceed with building gliders with good success and some sales. I instructed buyers of my gliders in how to fly them and also interested students to learn to fly them. I also advertised for experimental airplane work for others and by 1906 established the first airplane manufacturing plant in my laboratory and made aviation my business.

By the time this ad appeared in a 1917 magazine, the final 'n' had been dropped from the name.

"This lead to the design and building of my first airplane, a bi-plane pusher type, completed late in 1907. To assemble this airplane and for the growing business, more space was needed. My brother Adolph joined me as C. & A. Wittemann and a much larger plant was planned and completed early in 1908, at the same address. My first airplane was then assembled. An automobile motor was used which had to be rebuilt to reduce its weight. When completed we made many short successful flights and gained much experience, which enabled me to design and build many airplanes for flyers at that time, with increasing success. Catalogs of airplanes, gliders, motors and parts were issued, which increased sales.

"At this time motors needed much development for use in airplanes. I found Gustav Whitehead of Bridgeport, Conn. was building airplane motors for use in his experimental airplanes. He agreed to sell me two of his motors, which I assisted him to complete and used them with reasonable success. Later other motors became available, the Gnome, Anzani, Eldridge and Hall-Scott. All were used with increasing success for the sale of my planes.

"William Aitkin became a professional Wittemann Glider flyer in 1907 and thru 1910 won prizes and cups flying our gliders.

"In 1908 the Aeronautical Society of America, was organized. I was a Charter Member and helped to organize it. The Society established a flying field at Morris Park, New York where flying meets were held in 1908 and 1909. Following that, the society obtained a field at Mineola, Long Island, N.Y., for the use of its members and to hold flying meets thru 1911. In 1912, with the co-operation of the Aeronautical Society, we established a new flying field at Oakwood Heights, Staten Island, N.Y., for the continued use of its members and for holding flying meets.

"During the year following 1907, I designed and built many airplanes for many of our earliest flyers, along with the many experimental machines that did and did not fly, including a helicopter for Lee S. Burridge.

"The largest early customer was Capt. Thomas S. Baldwin for whom I developed and built the many famous Red Devils he used for exhibition flying all around the United States, China, Japan and India.

"In addition, I carried on many experiments with airplanes, gliders, rigid and variable pitch wood, steel and aluminum propellers, helicopters, steam engine driven model planes and many other airplane developments. During these years I taught some and helped other early flyers learn to fly airplanes.

"In 1912 I needed more space and added an extension to my plant, doubling its floor space and making the assembly area 110 feet long.

"In 1914, Samuel Lewis joined me and the company was then named Wittemann-Lewis Aircraft Company and moved to a larger plant in Newark, New Jersey. There, I developed and built training planes, the first enclosed fuselage plane with pontoons and twin engines, test flown from Newark Bay, a pilotless plane for the U.S. Navy with Carl Norden instruments, and others.

"In 1917, President Wilson appointed me to the Federal Military Aviation Committee.

"A survey was made of the Newark meadows for the building of a modern airport but found the meadows would have been too costly to improve. Then a 500 acre tract at Hasbrouck Heights, N.J., now Teterboro Airport, was found more practical and in late 1917 built a new airport and plant there, completed in early 1918. That plant had an open span of 120 feet for building large planes. With that facility, I obtained a contract from the U. S. Army for the two largest bombing airplanes with six motors each, the largest planes built up to that time.

"In 1920, a fleet of DH-4 Army airplanes were re-engineered and re-built completely for initiation of the trans-continental U.S. Post Office Department, Air Mail Service, some of which were flown by such famous mail pilots as Col. Charles A. Lindbergh, Irving D. Lamb and John 0. Webster.

"Later I continued my research and development for large transport planes for maximum safety and flying range, in wind tunnels at M.I.T., Cambridge, Mass., Bureau of Standards, Washington, New York University, N.Y. City and Carnegie Institute of Technology, Pittsburgh, thru which I developed extensive engineering data.

"In acquiring the Teterboro Airport land, my plans for the final lay-out of the airport are more fully outlined on an artists sketch prepared in 1917 and 1918, which shows those thoughts were very much in line with the lay-outs of our modern airports.

"The development of Teterboro Airport was gradual. After first building my new plant, two runways were laid out and built to give ample landing and take-off facility. Recognizing the need of airplane landing and take-off control, the first airport signal tower of record, was built over the plant roof.

"I also have the privilege and honor of being a Charter Member of the "Early Birds of Aviation". Its main requirement for eligibility is, to have soloed prior to December 17, 1916, a Life Member of the "Silver Wings", Honorary Colonel in the Operation "Find It" Unit of the 9315th Air Reserve Squadron, Connecticut, Honorary Member of the "Connecticut Aeronautical Historical Association" Commission as "Admiral of the Flag Ship Fleet" of the American Air Lines, Inc. and now reside in Farmingdale, New Jersey."

        Charles Charter R. Wittemann
        Paynters Road, R. D. 2,
        Farmingdale, N.J.

October 26, 1965

A recently discovered French postcard of Wittemann in one of his aircraft. The card was signed and dated in 1906. No other details known about the aircraft, but notice it is a triplane with the vertical and horizontal control surfaces situated at the front of the aircraft.

A rare C. & A. Wittemann Catalog from circa 1910 can be found reproduced in its entirety starting on page 115.

Chapter 3

Richmond County Fair

Aviation was all the rage in 1910. In that year the Richmond County Fair had an aviation theme. The famous aerial performer Thomas Scott Baldwin was there and, of course, he did an aerial demonstration.

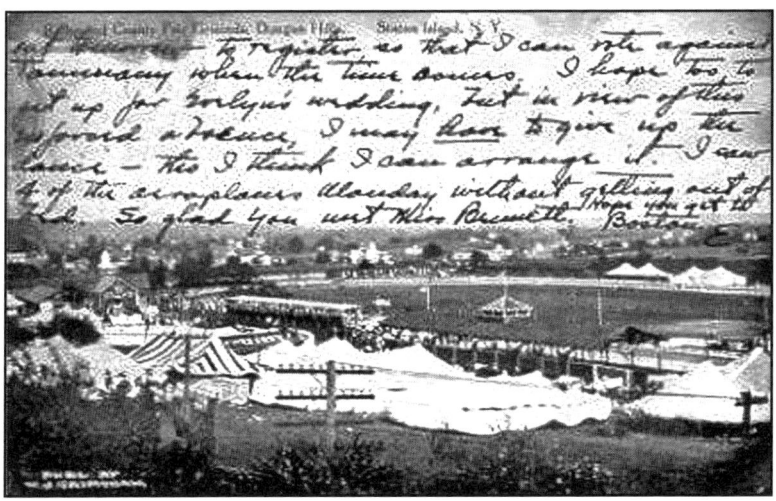

Postcard showing the Richmond County Fairgrounds.

Ted Lovington, a local Staten Islander, displayed his hydroplane, although it was still under construction and did not fly at the fair. By 1911 aviation had an even stronger foothold on the imagination of the local Staten Islanders. In that year, the famed aviatrix, Harriet Quimby, wowed over 15,000 people at the Richmond County Fair. She was the first woman to receive a pilot's license. She also became the first woman to fly at night, although some others are credited with that feat. She made the night flight that evening in front of the same crowd.

Quimby was to become the first woman to pilot an airplane

Harriet Quimby in a Bleriot monoplane.

across the English Channel, although it scarcely made the newspapers at the time. Her accomplishment was over shadowed by media coverage of the "Titanic" disaster. Her channel crossing was on April 14 of 1912. Just two days after the "unsinkable" "Titanic" went to the bottom of the Atlantic Ocean.

She made her channel crossing in a borrowed French Bleriot monoplane. She liked the aircraft so much that she bought a pure white Bleriot and had it shipped to the US.

Prior to performing in the third annual Boston Air Meet, as they called air show/races then, Quimby went for a practice flight in this Bleriot with the air show manager, Mr. William Willard. Mr. Willard was said to be somewhat overweight. Aircraft weight and balance

The Official Program from 1912.

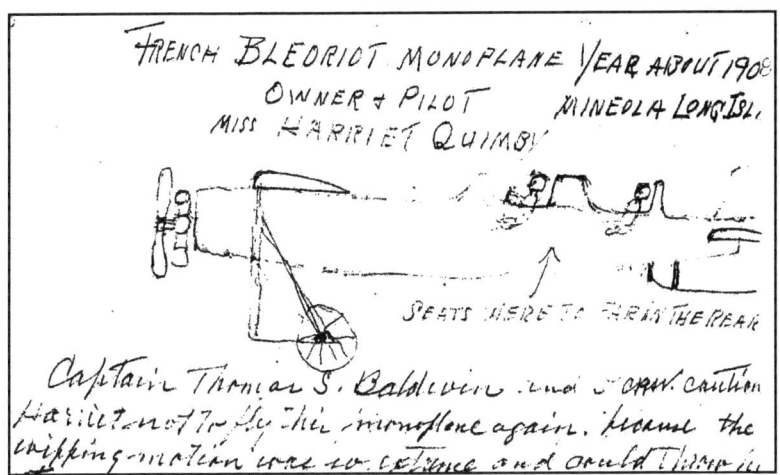

Charles Wittemann's hand-written sketch of the problems with Quimby's Bleriot, which caused her fatal accident.

limits were still a thing of the future at that time. During her descent the airplane pitched violently upward and stalled into a nosedive. She, along with the air show manager, were thrown to their deaths from this airplane. Aircraft seat belts were also a thing of the future. Their bodies were recovered by a launch from a local yacht club.

They were stuck headfirst in the mud under three feet of water in Boston Harbor. Witnesses said that the fall had been about 200 feet.

In Charles Wittemann's hand written notes he explains the fault in Quimby's aircraft and tells of his warning to her that she should not fly it because of this flaw. He explains that this problem would cause a violent pitching that could be dangerous. Of course, this is what caused the accident that killed her and Mr. Willard.

The note is faint and hard to read. It says:
FRENCH BLERIOT MONOPLANE YEAR ABOUT 1908
Owner & Pilot   Mineola Long Isl.
Miss Harriet Quimby
Seat here too far to the rear (arrow to illustration)
Captain Thomas Baldwin and I caution Harriet not to fly the monoplane again. Because the whipping motion was so extreme and could throw her out. NO HEED. At a Boston meet carrying a passenger Charles Willard. Both were thrown out & killed."

George Boyd flying his Rex Monoplane, probably at Miller Field.

(Although his note said 1908, it was actually 1912. Charles Wittemann wrote the comment from memory years later.)

In 1912 George N. Boyd flew for the Richmond County Fair at the Dongan Hills Fairground in a Rex Monoplane.

He flew five consecutive days to the delight of an estimated twenty thousand people. The Staten Island-built Rex Monoplane performed flawlessly for the duration of the fair. The Rex was almost an exact copy of the standard Bleriot, probably under license from Bleriot.

The fair grounds site was used as an ad hoc flying field for many years. The site was mentioned in the Staten Island Aero Club newsletter in the late forties.

The site of the old fairgrounds now supports a New York City housing project, a city park and hundreds of residential homes.

The site of the Richmond County Fairgrounds is now occupied by the Berry Homes apartments, private homes, and a city park.

Chapter 4

Confusion: Baldwin, Baldwin, White Wing, Red Wing, Red Devil, and Ailerons

Thomas Scott Baldwin and Frederick "Casey" Baldwin have often been confused with each other. Their roles in early aviation were almost parallel. Thomas Scott Baldwin was involved with the Aeronautical Society of America and Frederick "Casey" Baldwin with the Aerial Experimental Association. Frederick Baldwin, as part of the AEA, was involved in building a "Red Wing" and a "White Wing", while Captain Thomas Baldwin (along with the Wittemann Brothers) built a "Red Devil".

The driving force behind the AEA was Alexander Graham Bell. Bell formed this organization along with Frederick "Casey" Baldwin, John McCurdy, Glen H. Curtiss and Lt. Thomas Seifridge, with the objective of furthering aviation research. Curtiss had not yet begun to build airplanes at that time, his interest being motorcycles and motorcycle engines that would later lend themselves to aircraft.

It's also believed that Bell's wife funded the whole AEA project.

Frederick Baldwin and the AEA are often credited with the first use of ailerons, and in fact that was their case in the Wright/Curtiss lawsuit, Curtiss claimed that ailerons were a different concept and, therefore, the Wright patient didn't cover the Curtiss airplane. However, aircraft built by Charles Wittemann had functional ailerons long before the AEA aircraft were built. The Frenchman Henri Farman also claimed to have invented the aileron, again, this was after the Wittemann airplane flew. The AEA was granted a patent on ailerons in 1911.

The AEA is not relevant to this book except in the crossover with Curtiss and their part in the great Wright/Curtiss patent lawsuits, and of course, the confusion with Thomas Scott Baldwin and Frederick (Casey) Baldwin. Both Baldwins spent a lot of time at the

Hammondsport Airfield and both were close friends of Glen Curtiss, adding to the confusion. Thomas Scott Baldwin lived on Staten Island during part of the first decade of the century

As mentioned in the Wittemann chapter, there is some confusion about the site of the construction of the first Baldwin "Red Devil."

Mr. Henry Woodhouse, a prominent aviation figure in the first quarter of the 20th century, interviewed Mr. Leo Stevens, a close friend of Baldwin and one who knew all about the "Red Devil." Stevens said that he often visited the building at Oakwood Heights and the first "Red Devil" was built there. Stevens also said, "He built his first one at Hammondsport." When Stevens was reminded of this he said "that's alright, whenever Baldwin changed the design, or smashed it up he had to build it over." In "Outing Magazine", December, 1913, Arnold Kruckman said of Baldwin's "Red Devil", "He built the machine at Mineola, Long Island. The papers announced it as a second or third "Red Devil." He did a lot of experimental work

A recent photo of Hammondsport Airport.

on it and made some trial flights before he got it in shape. Some of this was done at Hammondsport, I know, and perhaps some at Mineola: But the "Red Devil" was actually and finally built in the building on the beach at Oakwood."

In "The American Magazine for Aeronautics" of 1911: "The new biplane of Capt. Thomas S. Baldwin, "Red Devil III" is a simplified and standardized replica in the main, of his two previous machines. The parts were built for Capt. Baldwin to his designs by C. and A. Wittemann of Staten Island."

The AEA "White Wing" and "Red Wing" aircraft were built in 1908 and the first Baldwin "Red Devil" in 1910.

Another historic misconception is that Lt. Thomas Selfridge was the first man to fly supported by a kite. Several of the Wittemann brothers (and possibly one sister) had flown this way as early as 1900. Selfridge did have the unfortunate distinction of becoming the first human to die in an airplane accident. That was in a Wright Brother's aircraft with Orville Wright at the controls.

Lt. Thomas Selfridge. The first man to die in an airplane.

Chapter 5

Oakwood Heights Airport

At the site of Thomas Scott Baldwin's aircraft shop, the Aeronautical Society of America, in association with another Wittemann brother, Harold E. Wittemann, built a new flying field. They added hangars and for several years it was known as "The Oakwood Heights Airport". The hangars abutted Mill Road.

The Oakwood Heights Airport as it appears today. Most of the area is unchanged. It became protected wetlands before the recent land boom. The houses on Mill Road encroach on the old airfield.

The New York Aero Club later used the Oakwood Heights Airport for both full size airplane and model airplane flying. Baldwin's original shop was neglected and eventually was washed into the bay by an unusually high tide. There is photographic evidence that the building survived into the 1930's.

Ruth Law often flew from the Oakwood Heights Airport.

Famed aviatrix Ruth Law gave exhibitions at Oakwood Heights in 1912 in a Red Devil aircraft. Wittemann built an airplane (another Red Devil) for Law, which she used in other aerial demonstrations. She went on to gain fame as the operator of a flying circus. Law, not yet a licensed pilot, was in Boston at the meet when Harriet Quimby was thrown to her death in the same year.

Harriet Quimby had also flown at the Oakwood Heights field.

Eddie Stinson, who was later to design and build the famous Stinson Aircraft, learned to fly at this Staten Island field. His famous sister, aviatrix Katharine Stinson taught him.

Harry Bingham Brown performed often at the Oakwood Heights Airport. Harry, with Isabel Patterson of Vancouver as a passenger, broke the altitude record of 5,280 feet (1 mile).

Arthur J. Laphem made several parachute jumps at the May 30 - June 1, "Carnival" and a military rifleman, Pvt. R. G. Sharotts shot several balloons while airborne. George Beatty, Charles K. Hamilton, Cecil Peoli and Ruth Law were at the same event. The "Stevens Safety Pack" was an early parachute system, developed by A. Leo Stevens.

Dr. Henry W. Walden, a member of the Aeronautical Society of America, flew his monoplane

Katherine Stinson taught her famous brother to fly at Oakwood Heights Airport.

The Walden Monoplane. Dr. Henry W. Walden was the "crazy dentist" of Mineola, Long Island. He is credited with building the first American made powered monoplane.

several times at Oakwood. It was this model, built in 1910 with a 40hp Hall-Scott engine and fitted with ailerons, that flew on August 3, 1910 to become the first successful U.S. designed and built monoplane. It was the first U.S. craft to be licensed by the FAI and the Aero Club of America (although credit is often given to its look-alike, the Walden III) This historic early airfield, except for a few houses on Mill Road, is now just a swamp. Protected by the Wetlands Act, it is likely to remain as it is for the foreseeable future.

A poster for one of the many events held at Oakwood Heights Airport.

Chapter 6

George N. Boyd

At the ripe old age of 21, just seven years after the Wright Brothers flew at Kitty Hawk, Staten Islander George N. Boyd built and flew his own airplane. The year was 1910 and George proudly posed for a photograph, shortly after flying his biplane at the Richmond County Fair Grounds, in Dongan Hills, Staten Island. This was truly a "home made" aircraft as he built it behind his home. This poor machine came to grief at the same fairground. Mr. Boyd, while doing a demonstration there, had a misunderstanding with a tree. While he was unhurt and the tree survived, the frail flying machine did not.

George N. Boyd

George Boyd and his biplane, circa 1910.

Boyd's homebuilt biplane after crashing on the Richmond County Fairgrounds.

Two years later, in 1912, Boyd flew at the same site, again, for the Richmond County Fair. His airplane this time was a little more sophisticated, being a factory built Rex Monoplane.

The Rex Monoplane aircraft was of the type designed by Bleriot in France; this example was built at the Rex Airplane Factory, in the South Beach area of Staten Island.

Unlike later aircraft, this one still had warping wings rather than ailerons. It also had a large wooden steering wheel instead of the levers common to the type.

Boyd was a test pilot for the Rex Monoplane Company and may have been a designer with them.

While there is no record of the Rex Company building a biplane, Rex had formerly been the Boreland Aeroplane and Motor Company. The Boreland compa-

This photo of a Rex Biplane is the only one known to me. The original caption says "Rex Biplane, Nassau Blvd.". It is believed that Boyd was the pilot.

Frontal view of the Rex Monoplane.

ny was started by Staten Islander F.H. Skinner. The biplane shown might have been one of several gliders that Skinner later converted to powered aircraft. I haven't been able to uncover information on this aircraft. The photo (although damaged) is the only one that I've ever seen.

When he married about five years later, his new bride, the former Alberta Gorman, convinced him to give up flying. Boyd never again piloted an airplane.

Mr. Boyd later lived with his family on Hart Boulevard, the same residential street that the famous aircraft designer, G. M. Bellanca would live on in the twenties.

This hangar on Staten Island was used by Boyd in circa 1912. It may have become the Rex airplane factory. Harry N. Atwood was an early aviator who often flew in New York.

Chapter 7

Ted Lovington

Ted Lovington built his first airplane long before World War I. This aircraft was a "hydro-plane" or "hydro-aeroplane" as seaplanes were then called.

He and his brothers, Joseph, Leon and John, toiled on the Johnson farm and estate that was located between Elm Park and Port Richmond, not far from where the Bayonne Bridge stands today. The aircraft's construction began in 1910 and even though it was unfinished, it was displayed at the Richmond Country Fair that year.

Ted's brother Joseph stands next to the float for the hydro-aeroplane outside the Johnson house on Nicholas Ave, Staten Island, in August 1912. It was built by brothers Joseph, Julius, and Ted (Theodore).

Theodore Lovington Jr., Ted's son, who still resides in Port Richmond, told me, "My father loved airplanes all of his life and flew in a flying circus after the Great War".

This "Flying Circus" was "Shaw Flyers". Formed by Commander George Shaw and Eddie Stinson (later, designer of the Stinson airplanes). Ted Lovington was a pilot/wing walker for the group and George Bradford was another pilot. Another Staten Islander, Ernie Decker, was an announcer and mechanic for the Flyers.

During the Shaw Flyers' time on Staten Island they used a field now bordered by Bard Avenue, Whitwood Avenue, and Davis Avenue. The area was, and still is, called

Sunset Hill. It was not really an airport but a flying field, never the less.

Lovington at one time worked as a wing walker for the famous barnstormer, Lieutenant Joe Ben Lievre. These two men, in front of a large Texas crowd, changed seats in a biplane, not an easy feat then or now.

According to Ted Lovington Jr., during prohibition the

The wings for the hydro-aeroplane in an August 1912 photo.

Shaw Flyers went into the profitable business of rum running. They acquired a flying boat and flew from Canada to Maine, and on occasion to Detroit. The "Flyers" kept many a speakeasy supplied.

Lovington also gained fame when he, Eddie Stinson and Captain

The completed hydro-aeroplane on Johnson's Field. The aircraft is displayed on mock floats. On the original photo the word "Dreadnought" is barely readable on the aircraft's rudder. The building in the background is a linseed oil factory which was later a storage site for the Manhattan Project (the atomic bomb which ended WWII). The area is still mildly radioactive.

Eddie Rickenbacker flew a German Junkers aircraft from Washington D.C. with a planned destination of San Francisco. Unfortunately they didn't make it. The airplane crashed in Omaha, Nebraska.

This was a ceremonial flight and they were carrying a letter from President Warren G. Harding to the Shriners Convention there.

Lovington was to complain of injuries from that crash for the rest of his life. The Junkers was said to be the first all metal aircraft ever flown in the United States.

Lovington, again in partnership with Stinson, opened an airline service from Erie, PA to Cleveland, OH.

He was also instrumental in coaxing C.M. Bellanca to move to Staten Island and to open an airplane factory there.

Mr. Lovington passed away in a New York hospital in 1965.

Ted's mother (Julia) in the rear cockpit on the day of her first airplane ride, from Staten Island to Connecticut.

Shaw Flyers at Sunset Hill. The hand written caption on the original says "Just arrived from Mitchel Field, L.I." "West New Brighton, S.I."

At that time he told his son that one of his last little pleasures was watching, from his hospital room, as a small yellow seaplane flew onto and off of Manhattan's East River.

A crowd surrounds a Curtiss 'Jenny' of the Shaw Flyers on Sunset Hill in 1922.

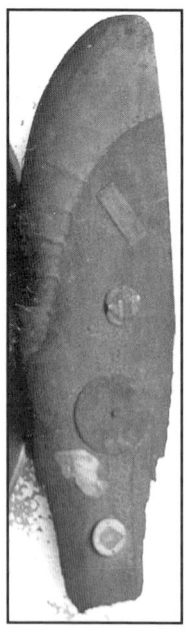

The broken propeller tip from a Curtiss 'Jenny' which crashed at Sunset Hill near Bard Avenue in 1922.

The prop from a Hall-Scott engined Standard airplane which flew from Staten Island Airport, circa 1927.

Chapter 8

The Unsolved Mystery of Bert Jewell

Albert (Bert) S. Jewell, a Cleveland, Ohio electrical contractor, was doing work in the northeast. His work brought him to Staten Island and while working on the island he fell in love. He lived at the Harbor Hotel, in Mariner's Harbor, Staten Island and there met Charlotte Carey, the beautiful niece of the hotel owner. She returned his affections.

William Carey, the hotel owner, also owned the Harbor Theatre and several storefronts in the area. Jewell later owned and operated a tobacco shop in one of the Mariner's Harbor storefronts that was owned by William Carey. The shop was located just across Harbor Road from the Harbor Hotel on Richmond Terrace.

While his vocation at that time had changed from electrician to tobacco shop owner, his real love was the excitement of aviation and airplanes.

Bert Jewell, circa 1908.

He landed a job as a test and demonstration pilot for the Moisant Airplane Company of Long Island.

While working for Moisant he would have flown with such pioneers as Harriet Quimby and Matilde Moisant. The first and second women to receive their pilots license in the U.S.

On October 19, 1913 Bert was scheduled to fly an air race from the Oakwood Heights Airport, around some prominent New York landmarks, including the Statue of Liberty, and return.

45

Bert Jewell (third from left) in front of his tobacco shop, circa 1912.

He took off from the Moisant factory field on Long Island (later Roosevelt Flying Field) in a Moisant (Bleriot) monoplane and simply was never seen again.

An extensive search, covering the nearby Atlantic Ocean, Brooklyn, the New Jersey Shore adjacent to Staten Island and the Narrows, revealed no wreckage. His route would have taken him over land to the Narrows, across less than two miles of water and along the Staten Island coast to the Oakwood Heights field, where the race was to begin. The newspapers of the time claimed he had been "blown out to sea".

The rumor mill was rampant.

One rumor played on his connections to the Moisant company. The Moisant Aircraft Company sponsored the Moisant International Aviators, a touring company that both demonstrated and sold Moisant Aircraft. The Moisant International Aviators toured the entire United States and parts of Mexico. The Moisant brothers were known for dabbling in international political intrigue. John Moisant had been a wealthy plantation owner in El Salvador. During a tour of Mexico they demonstrated their monoplanes in Mexico City, and later became involved in observation missions for the Mexican Army. They were rumored to be supplying aircraft and training for the Mexican Army during the Mexican Revolution. John Hector Warden, a Moisant pilot, was an honorary Captain in the Mexican

Alberrt Jewell in a Benoist biplane with a Roberts engine, circa 1912. I've seen this photo attributed to Janus, but this original was in the Jewell/Davis family album.

Federales. It's alleged that both sides were, at one time or another, supplied by Moisant.

When John Moisant died on December 31, 1910 his brother Alfred, along with his sister, Matilde, took control of the company and the Moisant Flyers organization.

At one time during the Flyers tour, the rebels surrounded the entire troupe and they had to be rescued by regular troops. The organization alluded to the troupe flying out of danger, but this was a fabrication to enhance their reputation. Allegedly Moisant aircraft and Moisant pilots acted as observers and bombed regularly during the revolution. This caused many historians, and some Staten Islanders, to believe that Jewell simply left his wife, children, and home, for a life of adventure in war torn Mexico.

There was one article in the Knoxville (Tenn.) Journal and Tribune that seems to debunk the later life of Albert Jewell. I was not able to find any similar article in any New York newspapers. The article, bylined "Knoxville, Tennessee, January 5, 1914" is as follows:

"Aviator's Body is Cast Ashore"

New York, January 4 - The torso of a body, believed by the police to be that of Albert J. Jewell, an aviator who disappeared while making a flight in a monoplane October 13, was cast up by the sea at Edgemore, L. I., today. It was not possible to identify the body positively.

Jewell left the aviation field at Hempstead Plains early in the morning, intending to fly to Staten Island to take part in a flight around Manhattan Island. He was last seen above Edgemere, ap-

Albert Jewell with his Moisant (Bleriot) Monoplane.

parently being carried out to sea by a strong wind."

I have flown this route many times, albeit in much more powerful equipment than Jewell's Moisant/Bleriot. It just does not make sense for him to fly over Edgemere. The probable route would take him over what is now Kennedy International Airport and on to the Narrows. I also believe that a powered fixed wing aircraft would not be "blown out to sea." I believe that this is a newspaper term left over from the balloon era.

Years later, there were even rumors that he was flying combat with the "Flying Tigers" in World War II.

Jewell's family investigated all of these rumors as much as their means allowed. They even wrote to the War Department, but nothing ever came of the investigation.

It is food for thought - a young tobacco store owner with dreams of adventure, the company that he worked with deeply involved in a convenient revolution. It could have happened that way.

Chapter 9

Miller Field

The Vanderbilt family owned more than one estate on Staten Island. The family farm was a three hundred fifty-acre plot on the west side of New Dorp Lane, bordered by Hylan Blvd., and the lower NY Bay. The Commodore's eldest son, William H. Vanderbilt, owned and lived on the property. He had discontinued farming and turned the property into a fairground, one of several on the Island.

In 1919, the U.S. Government purchased the land for use as a base for army aviation. The facility was named after Captain James Ely Miller. Captain Miller was the first American pilot killed in combat during the Great War.

The Vanderbilt tower stood long before the army took over the field. The stone tower held the water supply for the estate and it was an observation gazebo for the family. The tower overlooked the racetrack and had an excellent view of the ocean. There was a small kitchen within the tower so the servants could make snacks for the guests. Beginning in January 1936 the tower and the estate house were removed by WPA workers and a small pond was filled in. The removal of the 75 foot high landmark was a great relief to the pilots of the 27 Division Aviation, New York National Guard.

Tom Andrews, who lived

The Vanderbilt Tower, on the future site of Miller Field.

A Burgess-Dunne at Miller Field, circa 1919.

adjacent to Miller Field for most of his life, remembers the army blowing up the Vanderbilt Tower. Even though it was a WPA project, the army did the explosive demolition. Despite all the precautions the blast managed to toss a stone block over a quarter mile and maim a soldier. The tower had stood for over 50 years and the walls were several feet thick.

The field had a single North-South turf runway with a short paved overrun on the water or south end of the field. It also had a concrete seaplane (or hydroplane as they were then called) ramp. As late as 1993 the ramp was still there, albeit under the sand. It could be seen after a nor'easter stripped the sand away in 1993. It was covered over by sand again almost immediately. There was a pier on the southeast corner of the property. This was used both for seaplanes and as a docking site for the government owned lighthouse supply vessels. The pilings are still visible.

There is also an observation tower at the south end of the field overlooking the bay. The tower is of massive concrete construction and has slits for the sentry and/or gun director to look out toward the sea. This was built during World War II as an observation post for the artillery located on the field.

The Observation Tower at Miller Field as it appeared in 2003. Waiting for an enemy that never came.

Miller Army Air Field circa 1930. The Vanderbilt house is still visible in the center of the field. It was demolished in 1936.

This artillery consisted of "Anti-Motor Torpedo Boat (AMTB) 90mm gun M1 on mount model M3".

   At one time there was also a lighthouse built on the field. There was once a large elm tree on the site and early marine pilots used it as a landmark. Naturally when a lighthouse was constructed it was called Elm Tree Light. The light later became a two light marine

The Byrd Antarctic Expedition's Ford Trimotor at Miller Field.

51

range system and the aero beacon tower also supported the seaward range light.

Miller Field was to be the departure site for Charles Lindbergh's transatlantic flight, however the politics of the time made this impractical. Lindbergh did land there often, but not for his overseas flight. Admiral Richard Byrd also landed at Miller Field and used it as a staging area for his polar flights.

A New York Army National Guard unit on Miller Field in the 1930s.

Both Byrd and Floyd Bennett were regular visitors to Staten Island and were often seen in the local restaurants and became well known to the locals.

Miller Field was alternately an Army Air Force Field and an Army National Guard facility. At one time the base also supported coastal artillery.

Civil aviation was allowed to use the field on and off during its operational life. Bellanca used the field for the final testing of many of the CH-200 aircraft that were built on Staten Island.

Colonel Francesco DePinedo embarked on a good will flight for the Italian Government beginning in March of 1927. Before returning to Italy he would cross the Atlantic not once, but twice. Fascist dictator Benito Mussolini had encouraged and financed the flight. While the planned itinerary would take them over 40,000 miles, fate would interfere. They flew from Italy to Africa. DePinedo and his crew then flew from Africa to Brazil. They crossed the steaming jungles of the Amazon basin to Colombia. From Colombia they flew over the Gulf of Mexico landing near New Orleans, Louisiana. They traveled directly from New Orleans to San Antonio, Texas and then on to Hot Springs, New Mexico,

Colonel Francesco DePinedo.

The Savoia Santa Maria II being reconstructed at Miller Field.

landing on Elephant Butte Lake on April 4, 1927. DePinedo lifted off on April 6, 1927, after dumping 250 gallons of fuel, tools and spare parts to lighten the aircraft. Commander DePinedo and his crew landed at Theodore Roosevelt Lake, Arizona on April 6, 1927, at 11:50 p.m. The crew began to refuel the aircraft with gas cans and tragedy struck. A teenager carelessly tossed a lit cigarette into the lake. Gas had leaked from the refueling process and the aircraft went up in flames. Miraculously no one as hurt, but the aircraft was a total loss.

DePinedo called his friend, famed Italian aviator Italo Balbo, who in turn called his friend Benito Mussolini for a replacement aircraft.

Italo Balbo.

The manufacturer, Savoia Marchetti Aircraft, agreed to build an exact replica. This dismantled replica was placed aboard the Italian steamship Duiho and delivered to a Staten Island pier. From there it was trucked to Miller Army Airfield (National Guard at the time) to be assembled. Seventy Italian Fascist troops guarded the plane during re-assembly. DePinedo flew the aircraft back to Africa and on to Italy. Due to un-forecasted head winds, the Santa Maria II ran out of fuel some two hundred miles short of the mainland. The strength of the big catamaran flying boat was proven when it was towed the last two hundred miles by a ship. DePinedo then flew the Santa Maria II back to the site of the forced landing and finished the flight.

DePinedo later died in an attempt to fly a single-engine Bellanca across the Atlantic. The grossly overloaded aircraft ran off of the runway and the landing gear collapsed. DePinedo escaped the wreckage and went back to shut off the racing engine. The big Bellanca exploded and DePinedo was engulfed in the fireball.

On May 18, 1938 George Schaaf, founder of Richmond Airways, became the pilot of the first air mail flight from Staten Island. He took off from Miller Field at 1 am for the short but historic flight to Newark Airport. An air mail stamp cost six cents in 1938. Eight thousand stamps were sold for the commemorative flight and all had special postmarks with the words "First Flight". These stamps were the first bicolored air mail stamps ever issued. George Schaaf was a well known Staten Island flyer and his feats are chronicled elsewhere in this book.

In the 50's Nike missiles were repaired at the field. I remember, as a child, seeing the huge (to a small boy) missiles being trucked in and out of the facility.

The wreckage of the TWA Lockheed Constellation which crashed onto Miller Field in 1960.

On the sixteenth of December 1960 two commercial airliners collided over the field. TWA Flight 266, a Lockheed Constellation, collided with United Flight 825, a pure jet. The TWA aircraft broke into three major pieces and thousands of smaller pieces before coming to rest, mostly on the airport. Engines, luggage, aluminum chunks and body parts landed on the field and the surrounding residential

A 2003 photo of Miller Field, now part of the Gateway National Recreation Area. Note remains of the seaplane pier in the foreground.

area. All 45 souls on board died. The United jet, enroute from Chicago, flew a few more miles into the Park Slope section of Brooklyn where it too crashed, killing all 128 people on board. At the time it was the worst disaster in U.S. aviation history.

After all of the commercial airports on Staten Island closed, local pilots soon learned that by joining the Civil Air Patrol they could base their aircraft at Miller Field. Staten Island pilots flocked in droves to join the CAP.

The commander of the Civil Air Patrol at the facility was Colonel "Tex" Rice. Colonel Rice only had the use of one eye and one arm,

My father's Cessna 190. I later owned the aircraft and put over 800 hours on it. Note the CAP emblem on the tail.

55

yet he flew a Piper Cub flawlessly.

I flew out of Miller field with my father in the early 60's. He belonged to the Civil Air Patrol and based his 1951 Cessna Model 190 there. This aircraft was a five seat, strutless monoplane, powered by a Continental 240 horsepower radial engine. Toward the end of the field's life as a military base Fort Wadsworth controlled it. Prior to 1960 Fort Wadsworth, located adjacent to the Verazzano Narrows Bridge, had its own small liaison strip. Andy Origila, former head mechanic of Staten Island Airport, remembers Army DeHavilland Beaver land planes operating there.

Miller Field was deactivated as a government airport in 1969 and in 1972 it became part of the Gateway National Recreation Area. Today several ball fields stand on part of the site as does a high school.

The beacon and remaining hangars in a photo taken in 2003.

Chapter 10

Giuseppe Mario Bellanca

One time Staten Islander, Giuseppe Mario Bellanca was born in 1886 in Sciacca, Italy. Bellanca was a math student in Italy but entered the aviation business when he moved to the United States in 1912. Before his involvement with Staten Island, he built his first airplane in Brooklyn. He built this aircraft in 1912 behind a grocery store, and proceeded to learn to fly it.

Later in 1914 Bellanca opened a flying school in Garden City, Long Island. This proved to be a successful venture and many early flyers got their start there. One of the most famous being Fiorello LaGuardia, who went on to be a bomber pilot in the Great War and, of course, New York City's future, and until Rudy Giuliani, most famous mayor.

Giuseppe Bellanca on the cover of the July 6, 1927 issue of *Time* magazine.

In a barter arrangement for flying lessons, LaGuardia taught Bellanca how to drive in his Model T Ford. Bellanca moved to Omaha, Nebraska and started an airplane manufacturing company there. He also met and married his wife, the former Dorothy Brown, while in Omaha. The company wasn't very successful, although the airplane built there held many world records. This aircraft was the Bellanca Model CF. One of the accomplishments of the CF, perhaps a foreshadowing of Bellanca aircraft accolades yet to come, was a world endurance record.

Bellanca Model CF.

During this period World War I surplus aircraft were available for next to nothing and the Model CF sold for $5,000.00, a hefty sum at that time. Except for a few sales to successful air performers, orders were few. This lack of sales doomed the company. The original model CF is now in the Smithsonian's National Air and Space Museum.

After the failure of the Omaha venture, Bellanca moved back east. The Wright Aeronautical Corporation in Paterson, New Jersey hired him as a designer and consultant.

This was in 1924 and the Wright Corporation wanted an airplane to use as a test bed and as a show platform for its engines. From the union of a Wright Whirlwind engine with the Bellanca aircraft design sprung the Wright-Bellanca WB-1 soon followed by the famous WB-2.

The WB-2 was built at the Wright plant in Paterson. In 1926 the WB-2 swept the air race circuit and flew, non-refueled, for 51 hours.

Someone in the Wright Corporation realized that they, as engine manufacturers, were now in direct competition with aircraft manufacturers, their customers. The managing directors decided to divest themselves of the aircraft manufacturing part of their business and stay with their main mission of manufacturing and selling aircraft engines.

Bellanca left the company at that time and, along with Charles Levine, purchased the rights to the WB-2 and the prototype aircraft. Bellanca, along with his new partner, opened a factory in an unused and partially burned out building on Richmond Terrace, in the Mariner's Harbor section of Staten Island. This was the site of the huge Downey Townsand shipyard. Charles Levine was not a pilot or air-

The WB-2 being refueled.

craft designer and apparently was the moneyman for this venture. The new company was called the Columbia Aircraft Corporation. The WB-2 design was redesignated the Columbia and the aircraft itself renamed the "Miss Columbia". The Columbia Company office was in Manhattan at 5104 Woolworth Building, but the heart of the venture was to be the factory at 3493 Richmond Terrace, Staten Island.

One of the most famous dealings of the Columbia Aircraft Corporation had to do with Charles Lindbergh. Mr. Lindbergh wanted the original WB-2 for his transatlantic attempt. He believed that the WB-2 was the only aircraft in existence that was capable of the crossing. He was told by Levine that when he had $15,000 he could have the aircraft. Lindbergh traveled back to St. Louis and somehow raised the money. After a long train trip back to NY, Lucky Lindy plopped a $15,000 check down on Mr. Levine's desk and asked for delivery of his airplane.

As reported in Lindbergh's book "The Spirit of St Louis", Mr. Levine, in what must have been one of the worst business decisions of all time, told Lindbergh "You understand, we cannot let just anybody pilot our airplane across the ocean." Lindbergh, understandably, stormed out, went to California and had the Ryan Company build the aircraft that was to become the "Spirit of Saint Louis". Lindbergh and the Ryan monoplane took off for France from Roosevelt field at 7:52 am, May 20, 1927 and the rest, as they say, is history.

Levine and Bellanca did try to have their aircraft make the crossing before Lindbergh, but due to a lawsuit with the intended pilot, Lloyd Bertaud, the WB-2 sat in a hanger for the duration of Lindbergh's flight. Because of the controversy and lawsuit between Columbia (really Levine) and Bertaud, Bellanca issued a statement resigning from the Columbia Aircraft Corporation. This occurred before the factory actually opened, and the name was immediately changed to Bellanca Aircraft Corporation. The new factory employed between 50 and 60 Staten Islanders. Bellanca himself moved to Hart Boulevard in the West Brighton section of Staten Island. The aircraft that were built there were the next generation of the WB-2. This was the Bellanca Model CH-200. The CH-200 was almost identical to the WB-2 Columbia except for the landing gear and some creature comfort considerations.

The famous Bellanca Model K "Roma" was also built in the Staten Island plant. Built especially for a flight from New York to Rome, the Roma, with it's 65-foot wingspan, was the largest aircraft built by Bellanca up to this time. It was one of the first aircraft with

The Bellanca Model K "Roma" under construction in the Mariners Harbor factory.

retractable landing gear and was powered by a 550 horsepower Pratt & Whitney Hornet engine. The airplane was flown to Delaware for final tuning and testing for the transatlantic flight. In mid-summer 1928 the Roma was flown to Mitchel Field on Long Island, the planned departure for the flight. A lawsuit between the financing partners caused the flight to be canceled. The partnership was dissolved and in the end, Bellanca repossessed the Roma. The ship was later sold to Thor Solberg, who wanted to make an Atlantic crossing of his own. Norway was his destination. Solberg renamed the craft "Emma Jettic" and took off for his native Norway. The flight ran into adverse weather and didn't make it as far as Newfoundland. The Roma was lost to the sea but the crew was rescued. No other Model K's were ever built.

The original WB-2 was also almost lost during this period. The aircraft was fueled and ready to take off for Europe when it was "arrested" by the local authorities. The great weight of fuel had to be removed and during this operation a spectator tossed a spent cigarette into a fuel spill. The ensuing fire singed the paint on the aircraft but it did not ignite the dope on the fabric. The airplane survived. The "Miss Columbia" finally did cross the Atlantic. Scarcely two weeks after Lindy's crossing Bellanca's test pilot Clarence Chamberlain, with Charles Levine as a passenger, took off for Europe. They did manage to break Lindbergh's distance record and the flight became the first one to cross the Atlantic with a passenger. This flight terminated in Germany.

It is often written in articles about Bellanca that the Staten Island factory was located in Richmond Hill. There was never a factory in Richmond Hill. Bellanca did fly airplanes from a field in an area once called Richmond Hill. It was the future site of the Staten Island Airport. While the factory was located on Staten Island, Bellanca airplanes were tested at several sites, including Miller Army Air Field in New Dorp, Unxld Airport in Bulls Head, the Richmond Hill flying field and Hadley Airport in New Jersey.

In 1928 both Bellanca and the Bellanca Aircraft Corporation ended their association with Staten Island. Industrialist Henry B. DuPont, a friend of Bellanca, enticed him to move to New Castle, Delaware and build a factory there. Clarence Chamberlain moved with Bellanca and the two remained life long friends.

The original WB-2 was destroyed in a hangar fire in 1934. Only one of the Staten Island-built Model CH-200 aircraft sur-

Guiseppe Bellanca and Roger Kahn inspect the band leader's new Bellanca Model CH-200.

vives today. Dan Cullman is restoring it in Washington State. Roger Wolfe Kahn originally purchased this aircraft. Mr. Kahn was a band leader during the "Big Band" era. Recordings of his music are still available. Kahn later left the music business and went on to be a Fokker test pilot.

His airplane will fly again.

John Olson of Staten Island remembers as a pre-teenager meeting G.M. Bellanca and the workers at the plant. He would go there to "hang out". The workers saved him blocks of wood and other cut off pieces from the airplanes as play things.

When he visited the plant, a woman in flying gear would often greet him and always had a small bag of candy for him. Her name, as he remembers it, was Eleanor or Evelyn. I erroneously believed that this must have been the famous aviatrix Elinor Smith. Ms. Smith was a test and demonstration pilot for Bellanca and she was also his friend. Later I interviewed Ms. Smith and she told me that it could not have been her, as she never visited the Staten Island factory. Ms. Smith was in her nineties at that time and as sharp as a tack.

Mr. Olson also remembers George Fernic, not by name, but as the man who was one of the bosses there and who was killed in an airplane at an air show. Fernic, who is chronicled in the next chapter, was an engineer and aircraft designer for Columbia and later for

The fuselage of the only remaining Staten Island built Bellanca. This is Kahn's Model CH-200, now owned and being restored by Dan Cullman in Washington state.

Bellanca. Olson also remembers hydroplanes using the piers there and the big single-engine Bellanca airplanes being built. After the factory closed Olson still haunted the giant shipyard, and as kids will do, he searched for abandoned tools and such. He tells of being chased by rumrunners who used the piers, and being told to get out and not to come back. He still remembers that they carried machine guns, and he feared for his life. Olson says that during the great depression locals using two-man saws dismantled the piers and buildings of the abandoned shipyard and airplane factory to be used as firewood.

The uncovered right wing of Dan Cullman's CH-200.

Chapter 11

George G. Fernic

George G. Fernic had an engineering, ship building and aviation background. He was a ship designer and engineer first, but he had also studied aircraft design in Europe. He was also an experienced pilot.

He had been a Lieutenant (although his obituary credited him as "Captain Fernic") in the Romanian Air Force and saw action during the Great War.

Period newspapers referred to him as an "Industrial Delegate of the Royal Romanian Government".

He and his family moved to America and to their new home on Van Pelt Avenue in the Mariners Harbor section of Staten Island. Fernic came to the United States first and his wife Lola followed later on the Cunard Liner Ansonia. She was met on the pier by her husband. In a strange coincidence the Cunard Liner Ansonia was "arrested" with 7,000 cases of illegal whiskey on board. The vessel was later released.

George G. Fernic

Femic's father was a wealthy shipbuilder in Europe, and Fernic's first job in the U.S. was as an engineer for both the Staten Island Shipbuilding Corporation and the Townsand-Downey Shipyard Company.

R.M.S. Antonia, from a cigarette card photo.

He was also a designer/engineer for, and had become a close friend of, Giuseppe Mario Bellanca. G. M. Bellanca, who by this time was considered a master, may have greatly increased Fernic's skills in aircraft design. Fernic also worked in the Bellanca Aircraft Company plant on Staten Island.

Fernic's dream was to design and built an aircraft capable of the non-stop flight from New York to Bucharest. Mrs. Fernic told the press that her husband was going to have a passenger on the "New York to Romania" flight, and she was to be that passenger.

After Bellanca's falling out with his business partner Charles Levine, the Columbia Aircraft Company factory on Richmond Terrace re-opened as the Bellanca Aircraft Company. Columbia had never built an aircraft in the plant. Records indicate that Levine and Bellanca had their falling out before the lease was signed and it was the Columbia Aircraft Factory in concept only. This plant was in an otherwise unused massive building in the Downey Shipyard complex. When DuPont enticed Bellanca to relocate to Delaware, Fernic took over the rental space from Bellanca and bought some of the tools and equipment from the former Bellanca plant.

This factory was soon the birthplace of the Fernic T-9. Fernic's first original design, the T-9 had the look of many later Bellanca aircraft. It is possible the great Bellanca had learned some tricks from Fernic, rather then the other way around as is normally believed. The T-9 was begun in February, 1928 and rolled out for its first tests in May.

Fernic had another designer, Paul Dronin, working with him, either as a partner or employee. Dronin previously worked on the design staff at the Sikorsky plant in Connecticut, and later returned there. Fernic's father, as previously mentioned, a well-known, wealthy shipbuilder in Europe, funded this venture. The construction of the T-9 employed over 20 people.

The T-9 was the aircraft that Fernic intended to be his transat-

A regrettably poor quality photo of the partially completed Fernic T-9 in the massive factory on Richmond Terrace, Staten Island.

lantic flyer. It was a multi-engine aircraft with tricycle landing gear and streamlining reminiscent of modern business propjets. Two Wright Whirlwind engines powered the large aircraft. The T-9 was of composite construction. It had wooden box-type wing spars and the cantilever wings were of fabric-covered wood, but the fuselage had a tubular steel frame. His canard wing concept is used today on the commercially built Beech Starship and was used on Rutan's round-the-world "Voyager". Many very early aircraft, including the Wright Flyer, had canard wings. These were used as a balance much like the tailplane on a modem aircraft. Fernic's canard wing had the

Another photo of the T-9 under construction in the Mariners harbor factory.

stated purpose of preventing stalls. The forward, or canard, wing was built with a stalling speed just above that of the main wing. When the canard wing stalled, the nose of the aircraft would drop and the airplane would automatically increase speed in the ensuing decent. All of this would take place before the main wing stalled and would therefore prevent a "fall out of the sky" stall.

His tricycle gear system made for excellent crosswind capability and good ground handling. While tricycle gear is the standard of the world today, it didn't come into general use until the second half of World War Two. Virtually all airliners, military aircraft, and even the space shuttles have tricycle landing gear today. The so-called "conventional landing gear" has been relegated to bush and special purpose aircraft.

The ad hoc airfield near the Staten Island factory left much to be desired, especially for an aircraft as heavy as the T-9. The take-off weight of the T-9 was said to be eight thousand pounds. In 1930, just prior to his death, Fernic moved the Fernic Aircraft Company to Westfield, NJ. where a larger field and real runways were available.

Mr. John Olsen, an old time Staten Islander, remembers that the waterway behind the Mariners Harbor plant, known as the Kill Van

The Fernic T-10 in the factory at Westfield, NJ. Note the canard wing above the engine.

The Fernic T-10 in flight. Note the tricycle landing gear.

Kull, was used as a runway and many of the Bellanca aircraft that he remembers being built there were seaplanes. Both Bellanca and Fernic used the Unxld Airport that was near the intersection of Richmond Avenue and Jules Avenue. Bellanca had used both Miller Army Airfield on Staten Island and Hadley Field in Hadley, NJ for testing. In an unexpected move, the U.S. Army forbade the use of Miller Field for non-military aircraft and Bellanca was forced to truck his aircraft to an alternate field. Later the Unxld Airport became available.

The Fernic T-9 was too large to truck and with it's tricycle gear could not have been fitted with floats. It was towed to this airfield and further testing was done at Roosevelt Field on Long Island.

The second model, the Fernic T-10, was a much smaller aircraft with a single engine and a single-place cockpit. When the T-9 was damaged in a minor crash at Roosevelt Field, Long Island, it was put aside and the smaller aircraft was used for flight-testing. The T-10 had Fernic's signature canard wing and tricycle gear. It was to be a concept aircraft. Conceived and designed on Staten Island, the T-10 was built in the Westfield facility.

George Fernic traveled with his T-10 to the National Air Races at the Curtis Reynolds Airport in Chicago. This meet and series of races were held the last week of August 1930. Fernic was killed in the T-10 on August 24, 1930. He was given a military funeral by the Consulate General of Romania. American soldiers from Fort Jay, on Governor's Island, fired the salute.

The fate of the T-9 is unknown. It was dismantled after Fernic's fatal crash in the T-10, and the Wright engines were salvaged. Mr. Olsen, who had visited the factory in Mariners Harbor while it was in operation, says, "I was told by a worker that the big airplane was dismantled and scrapped in Long Island".

In her book, aviatrix Elinor Smith says "George Femic, a young Romanian flier, fell to his death in a plane of his own design that he had been trying to market as the latest thing in aircraft safety". Fernic had been attempting a loop just after take off. The underpowered (75 hp) aircraft fell out of the loop and onto another aircraft. Ms. Smith also said that Fernic was arrogant and would not have taken advice had it been offered.

Ironically, Fernic had witnessed the crash and death of Lieutenant John De Shazo just a few minutes before, at the same meet. A spectator was also killed in the De Shazo crash. Elinor Smith, James Doolittle, Giuseppe Mario Bellanca and an estimated forty thousand spectators witnessed these accidents.

Fernic's death ended the prospects for the ocean spanning T-9 and the Fernic Aircraft Company. There is no further mention in history of any Fernic Aircraft.

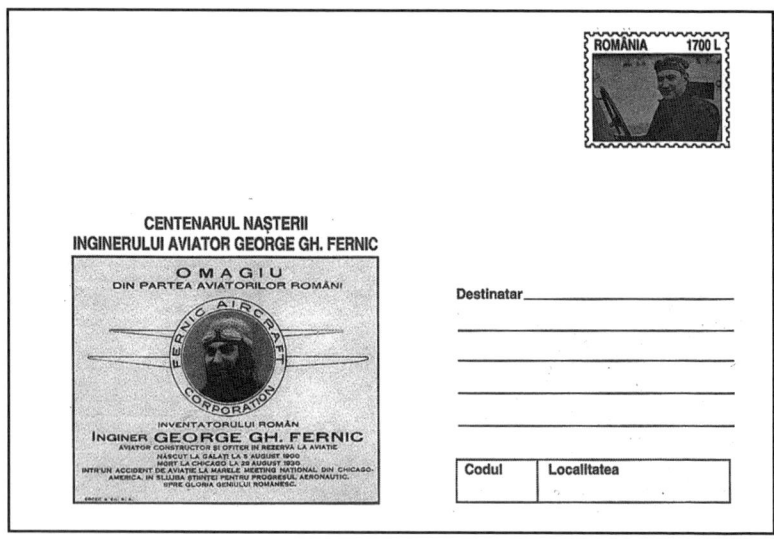

The Romanian government honored George Fernic with a stamp, shown here on the "First Day Cover".

The Latest Airplanes

Fernic T-9   *2 Whirlwind J-5s*

Fernic T-9 Tandem Wing

A bi-motor plane of radical design has been constructed and flight tested to the satisfaction of its designer by Fernic Aircraft Corporation, Staten Island, N. Y. The plane has a small auxiliary wing some distance ahead of the main wing at the fore end of the fuselage. In flight, the front wing stalls at a higher speed than the main wing, thus increasing the anti-stalling movement.

The landing gear consists of two wheels a short distance behind the center of gravity and a third wheel mounted at the fore end of the fuselage at an appreciable distance in front of the center of gravity. The front wheel, which is steerable, makes it possible to forcefully apply the brakes on the two rear wheels without danger of nosing over.

Specifications

Class: Experimental. **Type:** cabin, land, tandem.
Dimensions: Length overall, 41 ft. 6 in. Height overall, 13 ft. 3 in. Main wing span, 59 ft. Front wing span, 22 ft. Main wing chord (maximum), 10 ft. 6 in. Front wing chord (maximum), 4 ft.
Areas: Wings (incl. ailerons), Main 480 sq. ft. Front 70 sq. ft.
Weights: Empty, 4500 lbs. Useful load, 5500 lbs. Gross weight loaded, 10,000 lbs. Wing loading, 18.2 lbs. per sq. ft. Power loading, 25 lbs. per h.p.
Power Plant: 2 Whirlwind J-5s. Rated, 220 h.p. at 2000 r.p.m. each. Type, 9-cyl., air-cooled, radial. Fuel capacity, 900 gals. Oil capacity, 90 gals.
Performance: High speed, 135 m.p.h. Landing speed, 50 m.p.h. Cruising speed, 120 m.p.h. Climb (at sea level), 700 ft. per min. Service ceiling, 14,000 ft. Absolute ceiling, 15,000 ft. Cruising range, 4500 mi.
Construction: Fuselage, plywood bulkheads, spruce longerons covered with plywood and fabric. Wings, cantilever, U. S. A. 35 A modified airfoil section, box spars, plywood and spruce ribs, plywood and fabric covered.

A contemporay write-up of the Fernic T-9, with specifications.

72

Chapter 12

Fox Hills Golf Course

Fox Hills Golf Course was used in the 1930's as a flying field. It was a sprawling piece of land with enough space to support both the game of golf and the small airplanes of the time. The only records of this airfield are notes on the back of period photographs.

An early postcard of the Fox Hills Golf Club. The flat area in the foreground was used as the landing field.

In 1942 the property was taken over by the U.S. Government as an embarkation camp for soldiers going overseas. The flying field was leveled and a runway was built on another part of the property. Small army liaison airplanes used the field.

A little office was erected for communications with the airplanes and for a weather office for the pilots.

Later in the war the property was converted to a prisoner of war camp. The camp was used exclusively for Italian prisoners. The hospital at Willowbrook was used for German prisoners.

The runway at Fox Hills remained in army use until the camp was decommissioned after the war. The foundations of the barracks remained until the 1980's.

A Pietenpol on Fox Hills Golf Club/Flying Field, circa 1930. Buily by Adamo and claimed to be the first kit plane built on Staten Island.

The anemometer from the World War II Fox Hills military airstrip. The relic is owned by Francis Cardamone.

Chapter 13

Donovan-Hughes Airport

George Schaaf founded Richmond Airways in 1926. It later became Donovan-Hughes Airport. The airport was on the western side of Richmond Avenue in the Greenridge/New Springville section of Staten Island. It had a single north-south gravel/turf runway and several hangars. There was a seaplane base in the Fresh Kills adjacent to the airport. This seaplane base was considered part of the airport and was operated by Schaaf. There was also a seaplane ramp built at George Schaaf's home at the foot of Annadale Road, where that street meets Arthur Kill Road. There was a walkway through the swamp to the ramp. Mr. Schaaf often commuted to work at the airport by air.

Cornelius and Harold Vanderbilt, grandsons of the famous Commodore, had a unique seaplane built for them by the Kirkham Aeroplane and Motor Company. Although the company was headquartered in Bath, NY, the aircraft was built on Long Island at the old J. V. Martin factory. Vanderbilt built a ramp at his property on the west shore of Staten Island, near the Island of Meadow, and he also used the seaplane base affiliated with Richmond Airways. Kirkham

The Kirkham Air Yacht of 1925. Built for Cornelius and Harold Vanderbilt, it had a 450 hp. Napier Lion engine installed in a pusher configuration. Wing span was 47' 8". It could carry a load of 1820 pounds and had a range of 560 miles.

Aeroplane and Motor Company had merged with the Rex Airplane Company, late of South Beach. The great air yacht was lost in a fire in Vanderbilt's hangar at Port Washington, Long Island.

Schaaf operated Richmond Airways, Inc. as a sightseeing and charter company. The name Donovan-Hughes must have referred to an operator of the field at some time. Other than the airport name, I've found no reference to either Donovan or Hughes. Even the old timers who flew there have no recollection.

In the late 20's, Schaaf also had a factory on the field where they built and/or converted the Richmond Airplane. This aircraft is covered later in this chapter. George Schaaf learned his aircraft building skills while working for Charles Wittemann in his Ocean Terrace factory.

In 1942, the airport, along with the two other commercial fields on the island, was closed by order of the War Department for security purposes during WW II. All three civilian fields were allowed to reopen in late 1945.

Schaaf sold the airport in 1948 to Richard Gans, who operated it until its demise in 1952.

Their business card (circa 1950) offered a 15 mile ride at $1.50 per passenger and you could "learn to fly" for $60.00.

A handwritten note on the back of the card says "Valerie and her daddy flew over Annadale. Over Rita's, Pop's & Valerie's house in a Piper Cub". This little girl's note and drawing were written over 65 years ago. August Tornquist was the "Daddy." August still lives in Annadale.

In the waning years, the airport and its management supported mostly "week-end" flyers, unlike the more businesslike Staten Island Airport that was located directly across Richmond Avenue.

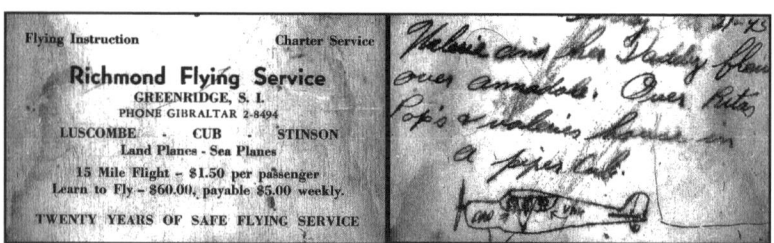

Richmond Flying Service business card. On the back is the hand written note from 1945.

In the 1950's there were many weekend "open house" celebrations there. These weekend activities included spot landings, where a circle was chalked in the grass and the competing pilots had to kill the engine on the downwind leg and land near the center of the circle. They also cut toilet paper that was dropped from another plane; the pilot who could cut it the most times won the contest. There were flour sack bombing competitions and, of course, airplane rides.

One of the local pilots, Eddie Bruder, owned a Piper Cub and flew with his boxer dog. The Cub has a right side entrance door that can open from both top and bottom. Eddie would fly the airplane from the back seat with the bottom door open. He looked out of the lower door and to the entire world it would appear that his boxer was flying. He would then land the airplane in front of the Sunday crowd of onlookers while an accomplice (my father) would tell them "See, it's not hard to fly, it only took that dog two weeks to learn".

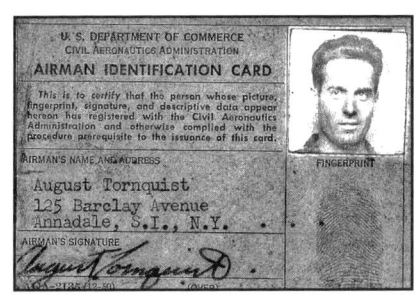

August Tornquist's Airman Identification Card (circa 1950).

Many Staten Islanders had their first airplane ride there, and over the years an estimated two thousand people went on to learn to fly. Jack (Cabby) Cabellero, who was a full time shop teacher in Tottenville High School, operated an airplane repair shop there. R. A. Martin's Flying Service was also on the field. Staten Islanders Greg Morgan, Jack Drury, Charles (Chuck) Gulino and Jim Drury all worked at the airport. Eddie Bruder was once the manager.

Gus Tornquist's Aeronca at the Donovan-Hughes Airport.

Greg Morgan still remembers Cabellero's 1946 Cadillac. It was the apple of Cabby's eye. Greg polished it endlessly. Greg's salary was 85 cents an hour. He was truly well paid for a high school kid in 1952.

Morgan also remembers

A rare photo of a radial-engined Fairchild at Donovan-Hughes Airport.

a brand new military surplus aircraft in a crate behind Cabby's hangar. He remembers it as a Norseman. The crate and the brand new aircraft were bulldozed when the airport closed. Chuck Gulino said that in the same period he earned 50 cents an hour working for Cabby.

Morgan related to me the story of a PT-19 that was being moved from Staten Island Airport, across Richmond Avenue, to Cabby's shop on the field. They placed a ramp over the curb for the plane to get off of the road. They waited until there was no traffic and

George Schaaf's Ryan PT-19. The pilot is Joseph Guido. This photo was taken in 1945 and the aircraft may be the same one mentioned in Greg Morgan's story. This aircraft was still registered as of June 2003.

An American Eagle biplane takes off from Donovan-Hughes Airport.

crossed Richmond Avenue, a busy street even in those days. The poor tired Ranger engine in the PT-19 just wouldn't put out the power needed to climb the curb, even with the extra push of a couple of human helpers. In the end they had to taxi the aircraft over a half mile to a level curb cut. Traffic was held up on that day.

Cabby had a pair of airport dogs. They were German Shepherds named Duke and Nomar. The dogs were classic "junk yard" dogs. While they were loose during business hours they ignored people, but when the sun went down they were vicious.

There was a hotdog restaurant called Jaynette's or Jay-net's adjacent to the field, and after flying, many pilots and instructors converged on the place for a "foot long" hotdog. A mile or so south of the field was the Almar Farms Restaurant, with the words "Long Island Duck" plastered across its front wall. Most patrons didn't know that the owner shot those ducks in the Fresh Kill Creek right behind the restaurant.

Left to right: Unknown, Jerry Crossen (motorcycle cop), "Cabby" Cabellero, Dr. Maibauer, George Schaaf, Jim Stamper.

After the closing of the airport in 1952, Gans sold the site to August ("Gus") Dinger, a local farmer, who opened an auto racetrack and a golf driving range on the property. Even though the airport was legally closed, Cabby's shop stayed open. Many an aircraft took off and landed on the auto racetrack after dark and many were rolled across the street from the other airport early on a Sunday morning. One day a man known as "Goldie" landed his Beechcraft Bonanza wheels up on the field. I don't know how they explained that, but Cabby got the repair job and it was illegally flown out a month later.

Shortly after the racetrack was opened the City of New York condemned the site to build a landfill. This landfill is part of the famous Staten Island dump, the largest in the world. The dump is closed forever, but alas, so is the airport, a sad ending for a great little airport.

The property is still at the same grade, albeit, crisscrossed with roadways, bulldozer tracks and a man-made water hole. No trash was ever dumped on this tract of land.

The property that was once Donovan-Hughes Airport. It is now part of the New York City dump. The berm on the right is there to keep the public's eyes off this land.

Richmond Airplane

There is much controversy about the Richmond Sea Hawk and Black Hawk. George Schaaf did build airplanes in his Richmond Factory. Cox-Klemin was the original manufacturer of the Sea Hawk, but this former military airplane was greatly modified for sightseeing work. A Richmond Aero Club newsletter (circa 1950) mentions both aircraft. The Sea Hawk was referred to as a modified ship and the Black Hawk as a Richmond Airways factory built plane. Both were true seaplanes and both took tour passengers for Richmond Airways. There may have been more than one Black Hawk built. The same periodical mentions Cornelius Vanderbilt (the famous Commodore's grandson) flying a Black Hawk, but it's unclear if he owned the aircraft or simply rented it from Richmond Airways. Aerofiles.com reports: "The Richmond Sea Hawk was refused re-licensing in 1931 as having "bad aerodynamic characteristics", and it was eventually parted out to various buyers."

The original Navy issue propeller from the Richmond Sea Hawk.

Chapter 14

Staten Island Airport

Staten Island Airport was the biggest aviation facility on the island. Used as a flying field since 1926, it was formally opened as an airport ten years later by Edward J. McCormick as a commercial aviation gateway to New York City. The field had two hard surfaced runways with a gross load limit of 45,000 lbs. The north-south runway was 3,000 feet long and the north-west south-east runway was 3,700 feet long and had landing lights.

There were five modern (for the time) steel hangers and plenty of ramp space. The airport carried ESSO gasoline and the ESSO name was embla-

Aerial view of Staten Island Airport, circa 1951.

Fairchild 24. This may have been the same airplane that my father flew to Guatemala.

83

A & E Flying Service hangar at the northern end of Staten Island Airport. The small lean-to section of the building was the home of the Staten Island Aero Club. The road is Richmond Avenue, near where the Staten Island Mall sits now. A & E stood for Anken & Engel.

zoned across the main hanger.

Edward J. McCormick, known as EJ by his friends, had a Fairchild Model 24 that he flew regularly.

On a personal note, E.J. McCormick and my father, John Drury, flew this Fairchild Model 24 from Staten Island to Guatemala in 1949, long before this type of trip was done in a general aviation airplane.

My father brought me a souvenir from Central America. It was a machete. I have no idea why he would bring his six-year-old son a machete, but he did. Years later he told me the story of that machete. It seems that they crossed the Central American Isthmus with only minor altitude problems. While in Guatemala, they bought souvenirs for relatives, including the machete.

The return trip was not as easy. The poor old inverted Ranger engine just wouldn't put out the power needed to clear the mountains in the hot, thin air. After several attempts to gain the necessary altitude they gave up for the day. That night they gave away their suitcases and most of their clothes. However, my father would not leave the souvenir he had purchased for his little boy. At four in the morning, to take advantage of the cooler night air, they again took off with hopes of crossing the mountains. He told me that they "rolled the wheels on the mountain" but made the crossing. They returned home many days later. When he gave me the machete, I, with my much younger eyes, noticed on the blade in tiny letters, "Made in Connecticut".

EJ also had a Republic SeaBee on the field and my father had a big 450 hp Howard DGA. I recall that he always said, "DGA stands

My father's Howard DGA-15 with a 450 hp. Pratt & Whitney. The house in the background is the Latanzio Kennels and farmhouse.

for "Damn Good Airplane". Doug Morgan, who worked at the Donovan-Hughes Airport across the street, said that when the Howard took off the windows in the building shook.

Bill Cullen, the TV personality, operated a charter air service on the field called "Appointment Airlines". This operated for about two years. The company used a few Beechcraft Bonanzas, including Cullen's own.

There was a very good-looking blonde woman who would accompany nervous passengers when necessary.

Arthur Godfrey and Burl Ives, both friends of Cullen's, also used the field on occasion.

Bill Cullen's Beech Bonanza (N3104V).

Staten Island Airport was home to the Richmond Aero Club. Some of the members included: Eddie Bruder, Lyman Decker, George Gluhasky, Nick (Nick the Russian) Vlsencko, Bill Skidmore, A.L. Picard, Carl I. Peterson, Jr., Ray Brinkerhoff, John Drury, Jake Molinoff, Art Kline, Ray Williams, Robert Link, John Diez, Cliff Knox, Dick Gans, Howard Sofield, R. A. (Ray) Martin, a man called Dutchie, and another known as "Horse Face" Charlie.

Andy Origlia was the head mechanic at Staten Island Airport for many years. He was also an accomplished auto racer. Midget racers were very popular in the late forties and fifties. Andy still lives

Andy Origlia and his midget racer. In the background is a Cessna T-50 (left) and a North American T-6 Texan (right).

on Staten Island.

Staten Island Airport closed forever on May 28, 1964. However, on August 8, 1964, Robert M. Mahoney of Phoenix, Arizona became the last person to land at a civilian airport on Staten Island. Mahoney, in route to the New York World's Fair, stopped at the site of the former airport for fuel. He was promptly arrested for landing on other than an approved airport. The runway was already partially destroyed, and Mahoney damaged his airplane.

The main Staten Island Airport hangar as it looks today. It was moved in the early 1960s and became an electrical supply house. It is now a child's party facility.

Staten Island Airport. Note the drive-in theatre at left.

Andy Origlia rebuilding a Stinson at his Rosebank, Staten Island home, circa 1946.

Piper Tri-Pacer at SIA.

Greenridge Auction Market located on SIA. It was originally the main hangar.

Andy Origlia props a Piper Cub for an unknown student, circa 1947.

Stinson at SIA, circa 1953.

Chapter 15

Richmond County Airport

Richmond County Airport or as it was commonly called, Travis Airport, was opened in the mid 1930's by John ("Honest John") Cosgrove, a prominent Staten Island attorney.

The western most of Staten Island's Airports, it was in a more rural part of the island. The airport shared property with the Alabama Auto Wrecking Yard. The airport's portion was 93 acres.

An overturned aircraft on the Richmond County Airport hangar, circa 1946. L to R: Anken, Engel, John Cosgrove, Andy Origlia.

To get to the junkyard it was necessary to cross an active runway. The airport was comprised of three unpaved runways and a seaplane docking area. Cannon Avenue, Glen Street, Victory Blvd and the Arthur Kill waterway bordered the site.

Paul Bullock remembers that he and his friend Billy Hawkins, both about 15 years old at the time, would pay five dollars each for a ride with Whitey, a flight instructor on the field. He would teach them to fly during the ride but if they wanted to learn to take off or land they had to pay a higher rate for flight lessons. Paul remembers the single runway and the seaplane ramp, although the ramp was idle when he flew there. This Instructor/pilot may have

Part of the Richmond County Airport site as it appears today.

been Whitey Walker, who later operated Cousin's Flying Service at Staten Island Airport.

The airport was closed and Cosgrove sold the land to the Consolidated Edison Company in 1955. The former airport property is now a Consolidated Edison Company power plant, and the site of the seaplane ramp is part of a paper recycling plant.

A circa 1950 crash at RCA. The pilot survived. The aircraft appears to be a Ryan PT-19.

A Cessna T-50 ("Bamboo Bomber") military trainer at RCA.

Mike Pallito proudly poses with his Stinson.

A Vultee BT-13 military trainer at RCA.

An Aeronca Champ rolls down the runway at Richmond County Airport, circa 1951.

Chapter 16

Aviation Locations on Staten Island

Bellanca Factory
Between Western Avenue, Holland Avenue, Richmond Terrace and the Arthur Kill. The site is now a park. The building foundation was still there as of November, 2005.
Longitude: W 74-10-53
Latitude: N 40-38-47

Clark Avenue Strip
Located about ¼ mile north of Amboy Road on Clark Avenue, behind the former "Ye Ol' Dutchman's" bar and grill.
Longitude: W 74.132663
Latitude: N 40.564587

Donovan-Hughes / Richmond Airways Airport
Directly across Richmond Avenue from the former Staten Island Airport. This site is now part of the Staten Island Sanitary Landfill.
Longitude: W 74-10-17
Latitude: N 40-34-61

Fort Wadsworth
At this location there was a small liaison strip, near the water, used into the early fifties by the U.S. Army. It was located near what is now the western base of the Verrazano Narrows Bridge.
Longitude: W 74.058495
Latitude: N 40.596749

Fox Hills Golf Course and Flying Field
Located adjacent to the military strip. Bordered by Vanderbilt Avenue, Tompkins Avenue, Targee Street, Steuben Street and the

Staten Island Rapid Transit Railroad. This site now contains a low income housing complex, a park and many private homes.
Longitude: W 74.080296
Latitude: N 40.614865

Fernic Factory

This is the former building and plant of the Bellanca Factory. Between Western Avenue, Holland Avenue, Richmond Terrace and the Arthur Kill. The site is now a park. The building foundation was still there as of November, 2005.
Longitude: W 74-10-53
Latitude: N 40-38-47

Gans (John & Herb) Seaplane Ramp

In 1918 John Gans (his son Richard later owned the Donovan-Hughes airport from 1948-1952) built a seaplane ramp and hangar at New Dorp Beach. The hangar still stood in 1950. They owned a Curtiss Seagull (a 3-place flying boat powered by a 150 hp engine).
Longitude: W 74.098492
Latitude: N 40.561678

Gans (Herb) Flying Field

Herb returned to flying with a Stinson landplane in 1920. The field that Herb used was on Victory Blvd, near Silver Lake, where the Golf Court Apartments were later built.
Longitude: W 74.09214
Latitude: N 40.624181

Johnson's Field

This field was bordered by Nicolas Avenue, the Staten Island North Shore Rail Line and Richmond Terrace. The field remains much as it was in 1910, although there are plans to build townhouses on the site.
Longitude: W 74-08-35
Latitude: N 40-38-34

La Tourette Golf Course

Utilizing the west side of the golf course (between the present No.1 tee and the No. 1 green) Carl Rache flew passengers from

this site in 1919 & 1920 in an Air King with an OX-5 engine.
Longitude: W 74.147501
Latitude: N 40.58228

Miller Army Air Field
This field was bordered by New Dorp Lane, Hylan Blvd and Lower New York Bay. It is now part of the Gateway National Recreation Area.
Longitude: W 74-05-54
Latitude: N 40-33-91

Oakwood Heights Aerodrome
Bordered by Old Mill Road, Kissam Street, the foot of Guyon Avenue and the Raritan Bay. The field is overgrown with reeds. It is now a part of the Gateway National Recreation Area. Except for the missing hangars and workshops it is largely unchanged since its closure in 1913.
Longitude: W 74-06-59
Longitude: N 40-33-19

Rex Aircraft Company
South Beach, Staten Island.
Longitude: W 74.068966
Latitude: N 40.590884

Richmond County Airport / Travis Airport
The Staten Island Con Edison generating plant now occupies this site. It was bordered by Cannon Avenue, Glenn Street, Victory Blvd and the Arthur Kill.
Longitude: W 74-11-48
Latitude: N 40-33-16

Richmond County Fair Grounds
Dongan Hills.
Now occupied by the Berry Houses (a New York City housing project) and McAurther Park
Longitude: W 74.10023
Latitude: N 40.586769

Schaaf's Home Ramp
At the end of Annadale Road.
Longitude: W 74.177113
Latitude: N 40.56396

Silver Lake Strip. (see also Gans Flying Field)
Later became the site of the Golf Court Apartments.
Longitude: W 74-15-29
Latitude: N 40-32-83

Staten Island Airport
This is now the site of the Staten Island Mall and other nearby retail shops. Staten Island Airport main hangar moved to Bloomfield Avenue.
Longitude: W 74-10-48
Latitude: N 40-34-93

Sunset Hill Flying Field
This field was bordered by Bard Avenue, Whitwood Avenue and Davis Avenue.
Longitude: W 74.105197
Latitude: N 40.62471

Unxld Airport
This field was adjacent to, and at the time owned by, the Unexcelled Fireworks Company. Bordered by Richmond Avenue and Jules Avenue. Part of the airport property is adjacent to the existing Baron Hirsch Cemetery.
Longitude: W 74.15617
Latitude: N 40.618806

Westerly Field
Former Saint Michael's Home.
George Schaaf flew a Jenny with an OX-5 engine in and out of this field. He crashed it there in 1919.
Longitude: W 74.187187
Latitude: N 40.563919

Chapter 17

Time Line

1856 - Captain Thomas Scott Baldwin born.
1875 - Baldwin's first hot air balloon flight.
1884 - Charles Wittemann born September 15.
1885 - Baldwin makes world tour including parachute jumps.
1886 - Giuseppe Mario Bellanca born.
1889 - George N. Boyd born.
   - Albert N. Janis invents the hydroplane.
1895 - Staten Island Flying Club formed.
1896 - Richmond County Democrat announces Staten Island Flying Club's 2nd annual meeting.
   - Wittemann starts building kites.
1898 - Wittemann airborne by kite.
   - Lt. R.E. Peary speaks at Prohibition Park before leaving for the arctic.
1900 - Wittemann builds his first glider.
1902 - Wittemann builds his first controllable man-carrying glider.
1905 - Wittemann factory opens doors as Wittemann Aeronautical Engineers.
   - Baldwin Airship Company builds airships for the U.S. Army.
1906 - First airplane rolls out of Wittemann factory late in the year. First powered aircraft on Staten Island.
   - Firm of C & A Wittemann formed.
   - Wittemann solos March 16, 1906.
   - George Boyd constructs homebuilt airplane.
1907 - C & A Wittemann builds a new plant. The first in America specifically constructed for aircraft manufacturing.
   - Lincoln Beachley makes an 18 mile trip in an airship from South Beach, Staten Island to Hell Gate, with a stop at Battery Park.
1908 - Aeronautical Society of America organized.
   - Society field acquired in Morris Park, NY.
   - First Society meet in Morris Park, NY.

- Baldwin asks Wittemann to design and build airplanes. (These became the "Red Devil"s.)
1909 - Glen Curtiss opens his factory.
- Second Aeronautical Society meet In Morris Park, NY.
1910 - George Boyd builds his first airplane with the help of E.H. Skinner.
- In April Captain Baldwin builds first airplane, the "Red Devil".
- Ted Lovington displays his hydroplane at Richmond County Fair.
- Wittemann installs engine in Burridge helicopter.
- Aeronautical Society of America moves its field to Mineola, NY and had a meet there.
1911 - Aeronautical Society of America meets in Mineola.
- Wittemann builds a Baldwin "Red Devil" at factory.
- On September 11th, at the Richmond County Fair, Harriet Quimby becomes the first woman to fly at night.
- Wittemann doubles the size of their factory.
- George Boyd solos.
1912 - Rex Airplane built in South Beach, Staten Island.
- Last Baldwin "Red Devil" built by Wittemann.
- Aeronautical Society of America establishes flying field at Oakwood Heights Airport, former site of Baldwin's shop and airfield.
- Ruth Law gives exhibitions in "Red Devil" at Oakwood Heights Airport.
- April 16, Harriet Quimby becomes the first woman to pilot an aircraft across the English Channel.
- July 1, Harriet Quimby dies in Boston crash.
- Richmond County Fair, August 7, 8, 9, 10, and 11. George Boyd flies Rex Monoplane each day.
- Giuseppe Mario Bellanca immigrates to U.S.
1913 - Richmond County Fair has an aviation exposition.
- Baldwin advertises "Red Devils" for sale.
- Albert Jewell lost October 19th while going to the "New York Times Aerial Derby" at Oakwood Heights Airport.
- Wittemann builds several Curtiss pusher-type aircraft.
1914 - Adolph Wittemann left the company and went to sea as a steam engineer.
- Wittemann Company reformed as Wittemann-Lewis Aircraft Company.

- late in the year Wittemann-Lewis moved to Newark Meadows.
- Sundstedt Hydroplane aircraft built in Newark by Wittemann.
- Staten Island Wittemann plant closed.
- Bellanca opens flight school in LI, teaches LaGuardia to fly.

1915 - Lovington flies hydro aeroplane at Port Richmond, SI.
- U.S. Patent Office confirms Janin's right to invention of hydroplane over Curtiss.

1916 - Wittemann-Lewis moves to Hasbrouck Heights, NJ and founds what is to become Teterboro Airport

1917 - Lewis leaves Witteman-Lewis. Name changed to Witteman Aircraft Corporation.

1918 - Construction begins on Miller Army Air Field.
- Charles Wittemann appointed by President Wilson to the President's Aviation Commission.

1919 - Witteman Aircraft awarded contract to convert military De-Haviland DH-4 aircraft to air mail configuration.

1920 - Witteman awarded contract for the largest aircraft ever to be built at that time (the Barling Bomber).

1921 - Bellanca moved to Omaha, Nebraska. Builds the model CF.

1923 - First of the large bombers completed by Witteman.
- Witteman completes DH-4 air mail aircraft contract.
- Wittemann's loses control of company due to failure of government overrun payment.

1924 - Bellanca works for Wright, designs WB-2.

1925 - Witteman Aircraft Company bankrupt, plant and field sold to Fokker Aircraft.

1926 - George Schaaf establishes airport later called Donovan-Hughes / Richmond Airways.
- Site of the future Staten Island Airport opens as a flying field.
- On December 2nd Sir Alan Cobham carries the first mail from Staten Island by air. Route goes from Staten Island to Philadelphia. Reported in the NY Times on December 3rd.
- Bellanca's WB-2 sweeps the year's air races.

1927 - Bellanca and Levine open the Columbia Aircraft Company.
- Bellanca's picture is on the cover of Time magazine.
- May 20th, Lindbergh takes off for Paris on first successful solo, non-stop flight.
- May 22nd, Bellanca splits with Levine and moves to Newcastle Delaware.

- Chamberlain and Columbia (WB-2) cross the Atlantic Ocean with Charles Levine as passenger.
1928 - Bellanca opens Bellanca Aircraft Company's Delaware factory.
- First Richmond airplane built at future site of Donovan-Hughes Airport
- In September Fernic opens factory on Richmond Terrace, SI. Builds the Fernic T-10.
1929 - Fernic and Dronin test fly T-9 at Roosevelt Field. Duration 22 minutes.
1929-30 - Fernic Aircraft moves to Westfield, NJ.
1930 - In July Fernic test flies the T-10 at Westfield, NJ.
- Fernic dies in crash of Fernic T-10 at Chicago air meet.
1931 - Miller Field is turned over to National Guard.
1933 - Ann Phillips becomes first woman to parachute on SI.
1934 - On January 25th the original WB-2 is destroyed by fire.
1935 - Miller Field returns to U.S. Army use.
1936 - Staten Island Airport formally opens. The flying field there was called Richmond Hill field.
- Richmond Airways airport becomes Donovan-Hughes Airport.
1938 - On May 18th, the inaugural airmail flight from Miller field takes off. Pilot is George Schaaf. (See also 1926.)
- Richmond County Airport (Travis) opens.
1942 - All Staten Island civil airports closed due to the war.
1944 - Staten Island airports reopen.
1948 - R & H Beer blimp is christened at Staten Island Airport.
- Donovan-Hughes Airport sold to Richard Gans
1950 - TV personality Bill Cullen opens charter airline at SI Airport.
1953 - Donovan-Hughes Airport closes.
1955 - Richmond County Airport closes.
1960 - Giuseppe Mario Bellanca dies.
1964 - E.J. McCormick's widow closes Staten Island Airport.
1967 - Charles Wittemann dies.
1969 - Miller Army Air Field closes.
1981 - George N. Boyd dies.

Chapter 18

Staten Island Aviators and Enthusiasts

This is a list of names of people I came across during my research that have some connection with aviation on Staten Island. Some are little more than names while others have some details. There are, of course, many more. Please contact the author if you have any names or further information that will help to finish this list or add details to the names already on it.

Adamo - Built and flew airplane at the Fox Hills Golf Club. (The golf course was also used as a flying field).
Adams, Louis R. - President of the Aeronautical Society of America (1912).
Anderson, E.D. - Director of the Aeronautical Society of America (1912).
Arcier, A. Francis - Worked for Charles Wittemann. Designed the Wittemann Barling Bomber.

Bang, Charles - Staten Island Flying Club member in 1895.
Beatty, George W. - Pilot, member of the Aeronautical Society of America (1912). Lived in Oakwood Heights.
Bellanca, Giuseppe Mario - Designer and builder of Bellanca Aircraft.
Bennett, Floyd - Personal pilot for Admiral Byrd.
Bitetti, Anthony - Built homebuilt airplane 1929. Mr. Bitetti worked for the Wright Aeronautical Corporation and helped build the Wright-Bellanca WB-1. He later worked for Bellanca and built CH-200 Aircraft in Mariners Harbor.
Boyd, George N. - Built airplane in 1910. Flew at the Richmond County Fair in 1912.
Boyd, M.W. - (1950)
Brinkerhoff, Ray - 100 Lindbergh Avenue, New Dorp, Staten Island.

Partial owner of a Luscombe. "Goofy" McDowell, a mailman, was a partner in the aircraft.

Brown, Harry Bingham - Member of the Aeronautical Society of America (1912). Lived in Oakwood Heights.

Bruder, Ed - Personal friend of Floyd Bennett. Former manager of Donovan-Hughes Airport. Later an Air Traffic Controller at JFK.

Byrd, Richard - Admiral and famed explorer.

Caballero, John ("Jack" or "Cabby") - NYC school teacher, also ran a repair shop at Donovan-Hughes Airport.

Cobb, Lee J. - Movie actor. Had a Waco Cabin aircraft at Staten Island Airport

Cosgrove, John ("Honest John") - Lawyer. Owned Richmond County Airport at Travis, Staten Island.

Crawford, Gustave - Later a helicopter pilot with the NYC Air Police. Trained the first crews in a Bell-47. Law enforcement award named after him.

Cusick, Charles - Staten Island Airport.

Decker, Rick - Also raced in the Indianapolis 500.

Deppe, Al, Jr - Owned the famous Al Deppe's Restaurant not far from Staten Island Airport. His wife's name was Wanda.

Diaz, John

Doyle, A. - Staten Island Flying Club member 1895.

Drennan, John - Restored a 1939 Fairchild 24. The aircraft still flies.

Dronin - Worked at Fernic Aircraft Company as a designer (1928).

Drury, John - Owned a Howard DGA 15 and a Cessna 190, based at Staten Island Airport.

Dubovsky, William

Dunham, Henry - Helped build new runways and hangers at Staten Island Airport in 1936. He got his pilot's license in 1938.

Dyott, George M. - Member of the Aeronautical Society of America (1912). Lived in Oakwood Heights.

Facciola, Al ("Gigi")

Facciola, Robert ("Bobbie")

Fernic, George - Opened an airplane factory at Mariners Harbor. Raced in the Indianapolis 500.

Gans, Herb - Had a flying field near Silver lake, at the site of the

present day Golf Court Apartments.
Gans, John - (Richard's father.) Built a seaplane hangar and ramp on New Dorp Beach in 1919.
Gans, Richard ("Dick") - Once owned Staten Island Airport (after George Schaaf).
Gardner, J.R. ("Robert")
Giamberdini, V.
Gluhosky, Frank
Gough, Herbert

Heering, Ray - Later a flight instructor at Morristown Airport. Had a DC-3 at Donovan-Hughes.
Hughes, James - Staten Island Flying Club member in 1895.

Jorgenson, Artie - Jorgenson Motors on Bay Street.
Jorgenson, George - Jorgenson Motors on Bay Street.

Kissell, E.
Kline, Art - Wrote Aviation News column in Staten Island Advance newspaper.
Knox, Cliff
Kowell, Ray - A welder. After not flying for 20 years he died in a homebuilt airplane at Colts Neck, NJ.

Law, Ruth Bancroft - Flew at Oakwood (1912).
Link, R.
Lovington, John
Lovington, Joseph
Lovington, Leon
Lovington, Theodore - Built an airplane in 1910.

Mahala, Charles, Jr.
Mahala, Charles, Sr.
Martin, Ray ("R.A.") - Owned a flying service at Donovan-Hughes Airport.
McDowell, Milton
McDowell, Walter
Meibauer, Conrad - Dentist.
Meibauer, Ethel ("Cookie") (nee Reiners) - Eloped with Conrad in an airplane.

Miles, Dr. Unice
Molinoff, Jake - Later owned a hardware store on Richmond Terrace, Staten Island.

Nielson, H.
Nolan, Jim - Joined the RAF before the United States entered World War II.
Nolan, Tom - Joined the RAF before the United States entered World War II.
Novac, Frank

Oberle, Arthur - Dentist in Red Bank, NJ.
O'Conner, J.

Peoli, Cecil - Pilot, member of the Aeronautical Society of America (1912).
Peterson, Carl - Crescent Chemical.
Phillips, Ann - First Staten Island woman to jump with a parachute (1933).
Picard, Alice
Porter, Russel - Died flying a commuter aircraft in Las Vegas, NV.

Quimby, Harriet - First woman to fly at night. First woman to fly across the English Channel. First woman to be granted a pilot license. Died in a Boston airshow.

Rache, Carl - Later a pilot for Colonial Airlines.
Rivera, Ralph
Robinson, H. - Secretary of Richmond Airways 1927.
Romain, Bill
Russel, P
Semler, Bob - Staten Island Airport.
Schaaf, George - Owned Richmond Airways and Donovan-Hughes Airport.
Sheridan, Leo
Sofield, Howard
Sohm, A. - Staten Island Flying Club member in 1895.
Springstead, Roy - Joined the RAF before the United States entered World War II.
Stinson, Eddie - Founded Stinson Aircraft Corp. Learned to fly on

Staten Island.
Stinson, Katherine ("Kathie") - Taught her famous brother to fly at Oakwood Heights, Staten Island.
Stone, I.F. - Made his first solo at the age of 62.

Thompson, J.H. - Staten Island Flying Club member in 1895.
Tobbacco, Robert ("Bob") - Rented Travis Airport from John Cosgrove. Later managed Marlboro Airport.
Tornquist, August - Staten Island plumber.

Van De Neyden - Treasurer of Richmond Airways in 1927.
Van Wert
Vanderbilt, Cornelius - The grandson of famous Commodore Vanderbilt.

Weinberg, Harry
Whitman, Woody
Wittemann, Charles - Soloed (1906). Opened the first airplane factory in the United States (1907).
Williams, Ray
Williams, T.R.
Wincapaw, William - Vice-President of Richmond Airways in 1927. Later Chief Pilot for Unexcelled Fireworks Company.

Chapter 19

Specifications of Some Aircraft Mentioned in this Book

Adamo (Adams) (Pietenpol) 1930
Henderson motorcycle engine.
Span: 28' 2"
Length: 28' 2'"
Useful Load: 395 lbs.
Built on Staten Island.
Registration Number: 742Y

Baldwin "Red Devil" 1910
50 hp Hall-Scott. Later versions had the 60 hp Hall-Scott.
Span: 28' 9"
Length: 28' 3"
Similar to Wright Pusher.

Beechcraft "Bonanza" V35
225 hp Continental, and others.
Span: 33' 6"
Length: 26' 5"
Seats: 4
Gross Weight.: 2,775 lbs.
Empty Weight.: 1,722 lbs.
Top Speed: 194 Mph
Cruise Speed: 184 Mph
Landing Speed: 55 Mph
Initial Rate of Climb: 1,300 feet per minute
Range: 775 miles
Ceiling: 19,000 feet
Take-Off Run: 500 feet
Landing Roll: 600 feet
Unique "V" tail, over 10,000 built.

Bellanca CH-200 (also known as the "Pacemaker")
Built on Staten Island.
220 hp Wright "J-5".
Span: 46' 4"
Length: 27' 9"
Load: 1,800 lbs.
Range: 700-800 miles

Bellanca Model K "Roma"
550 hp Pratt & Whitney "Hornet".
Span: 64' 6"
Length: 39' 1"
Range: 5,500 miles.
Load: 6,000-8,000 lbs.
Built for transatlantic crossing, New York to Rome.
Only one Model K was built. It was lost at sea in 1932.
Registration Number: NX4864

Cessna 190
220 hp Continental radial.
Span: 36' 2"
Length: 27' 1"
Seats: 5
Gross Weight: 3,350 lbs.
Empty Weight: 2,030 lbs.
Top Speed: 180 Mph
Cruise Speed: 165 Mph
Landing Speed: 63 Mph
Initial Rate of Climb: 1,210 feet per minute
Range: 750 miles
Ceiling: 18,300 feet
Take-Off Run: 1,670 feet
Landing Roll: 1,495 feet
In production from 1947 to 1954.

Cessna T-50 ("Bob Cat" or "Bamboo Bomber")
(2) 225 hp Jacobs.
Span: 41' 11"
Length: 32' 9"
Cruise Speed: 165 mph
Load:1500 lbs
Range: 750 miles
First built in 1939.
Military Designations: T-50, AT-8, C-78

Fairchild 24
200 hp Ranger inverted.
Span: 36' 4"
Length: 23' 9"
Seats: 4
Gross Weight: 2,882 lbs
Empty Weight: 1,813 lbs
Top Speed: 124 Mph
Cruise Speed: 112 Mph
Landing Speed: 57 Mph
Initial Rate of Climb: 730 feet per minute
Range: 465 miles
Ceiling: 12,700 feet
Built from 1932 to 1947.
Military Designation: UC-61

Fernic T-9
(2) 220 hp Wright "J-5".
Span: 59' 0"
Length: 41' 6"
Load: 5,500
Range as built: 450 miles
Range proposed for transatlantic crossing 6,000+ miles
Load: 5,500 lbs., NXI2OM
Built to fly nonstop New York to Bucarest, Rumania. Damaged in flight tests and never flown again. Carnard wing believed to be the first design for the "Stall Proof" concept.
Registration Number: NX120M

Fernic T-10 "Cruisaire"
75 hp Michigan "Rover".
Wingspan 25' 0"
Concept aircraft built by Fernic to prove systems while the model T-9 was being repaired. Fernic fell out of a loop with the aircraft, thus ending both Fernic's life and further development of the aircraft.
Registration Number: X9175

Howard DGA 15
450 hp Pratt & Whitney "Wasp Junior".
Span: 38'
Length: 24' 10"
Gross Weight: 4,350 lbs
Empty Weight: 2,700 lbs
Top Speed: 201 Mph
Cruise Speed: 180 Mph
Landing Speed: 67 Mph
Initial Rate of Climb: 1500 feet per minute
Range: 1,263 miles
Ceiling: 21,500 feet
Built from 1939 to 1942.

Piper J-3 "Cub"
40 to 65 hp Continental.
Span: 35' 3"
Length: 22' 4"
Gross Weight: 1,200 lbs
Empty Weight: 680 lbs
Top speed (65 hp): 87 Mph
Cruise Speed: 80 Mph
Landing Speed: 38 Mph
Initial Rate of Climb: 450 feet per minute
Range: 206 miles
Ceiling: 11,500 feet
Take-Off Run: 700 feet
Landing Roll: 800 feet
The "Cub" later had many engine variations.

Rex Monoplane
Copy of a Bleriot. It used wing warping controls and had a steering wheel rather than standard Bleriot levers.

Richmond "Sea Hawk"
160 hp Curtiss "C-6" pusher
Span: 46' 0"
Length: 28'
Load: 1,000 lbs
Fabric-covered wood wings, dural-covered wood hull; twin rudders. Although Richmond is credited as the builder, there is evidence that the first one was a converted Cox-Klemin military flying boat. This aircraft and the ones that followed were used chiefly for sightseeing flights over Staten Island and New York City.

Ryan PT-22
160 hp Kinner
Span: 30' 1"
Length: 22' 5"
Gross Weight: 1,860 lbs
Empty Weight: 1,313 lbs
Top Speed: 130 Mph
Cruise Speed: 123 Mph
Stall Speed: 64 Mph
Landing Speed: 54 Mph
Initial Rate of Climb: 1,000 feet per minute
Range: 352 miles

Wittemann Triplane
40 hp highly modified automobile engine.
Seats: 2
First factory built airplane in the United States. Said to also be the first aircraft with a swiveling tailwheel. Similar to a Wright Pusher.

Wittemann Barling Bomber
(6) 420 hp Liberty
Length: 65' 0"
Empty Weight: 27,312 lbs
Gross Weight: 42,749 lbs
Load: 15,437 lbs
Range: 335 miles
When it was first flown on August 8, 1923 it was the largest airplane ever built. Scrapped in 1928

Wright-Bellanca "WB-2"
220 hp Wright "J-5".
Span: 46" 4"
Length: 27' 9"
Load: 1,604 lbs
This aircraft beat Lindbergh's distance record. It was damaged in a hangar fire in 1934 and scrapped.

Chapter 20

Bellanca Aircraft Records and Accolades

1922 Bellanca Model CF swept the national and international air races, winning all 13 major races.
1923 Bellanca Model CF won the National Air Races efficiency contest at Saint Louis, MO. (This aircraft is now in the National Air & Space Museum.)
1925 Bellanca Model WB-1 won the National Air Races efficiency contest at New York, NY
1926 Bellanca Model WB-2 ("Columbia") won the National Air Races efficiency contest at Philadelphia, PA
1927 Bellanca Model WB-2 ("Columbia") established a new World Distance Record and the New York to Eisleben, Germany Record (two weeks after Lindbergh).
1928 Bellanca Model CH-200 (built on Staten Island) won the National Air Races efficiency contest at Los Angeles, CA.
1928 Bellanca Model J Pathfinder established a new solo world endurance record of 35 hours, 25 minutes. (The pilot was Royal V. Thomas in an aircraft named "Reliance".)
1928 Bellanca Model J Pathfinder established a new world endurance record of 59 hours, 7 minutes. (The pilots were Edward Schlee and William Brock, flying an aircraft named "Rosemarie".)
1929 Bellanca Model CH-300 established record for first nonstop flight From New York to Cuba, in a time of 12 hours, 56 minutes. (The pilot was George Haldeman.)
1929 Bellaca Model J Pathfinder established a record for a flight from Maine to Spain. The 3400 miles were flown in 30 hours, 30 minutes. (Pilots were Roger Williams and Lewis Yancy, in an aircraft named "North Star".)
1929 Bellanca Model J Pathfinder established a new solo endurance record of 35 hours, 33 minutes. (Pilot was Martin

	Jensen in an aircraft named "Green Flash".)
1929	Bellanca Model CH-300 established a new world endurance record for women of 26 hours, 23 minutes (Pilot was Elinor Smith.)
1929	Bellanca Model CH won 5 first place awards at the National Air Races.
1929	Bellanca Model CH won the Cleveland, OH to Buffalo, NY Efficiency Race.

Appendix
C. & A. Wittemann Catalog

FOREWORD.

OUR plant is devoted entirely to the manufacture of **Aeroplanes, Gliders and Accessories**.

We employ only the best of materials and labor. We warrant our machines and supplies.

In ordering, kindly mention the Catalogue page, the number or size of article. Goods are shipped at the purchaser's risk and by such conveyance as he will prescribe. Small packages can be sent by mail, when postage has been remitted. Articles and fittings, not listed in Catalogue, made or procured to order.

Remittances should be made by registered letter, in Express or Post Office money order or by bank draft. C. O. D. orders must be accompanied by one-third cash of the amount.

C. & A. WITTEMANN.

WITTEMANN BI-PLANE.

WITTEMANN BIPLANE

The range of control of our machines in both fore and aft balance is obtained by the use of pilot wheel and shoulder brace. The first when moved forward or backward governs the direction of flight upwards and downwards. The vertical rudder is operated by turning a wheel which governs the direction of flight to right or left. The shoulder brace moved laterally permits the operator to maintain his balance. The speed of the engine is controlled by a foot pedal, and the power can be shut off instantly by using the switch on the pilot wheel.

To stop when running on the ground a brake is provided.

Spring shock absorbers of a high grade are fitted to our planes to render starting and landing easy.

An ample factor of safety is allowed for, in all materials used in the construction of our machines.

Single or Passenger Carrying

Cover	Spread of Planes	Depth of Planes	Length fore and aft	Total Height	—PRICE—	
					Without Power Plant	With Power Plant
Double	30 Ft.	5 Ft.	33 Ft.	8 Ft.	$1200.00	$3500.00
Double	35 "	5½ "	35 "	8½ "	1600.00	5000.00
Single	30 "	4½ "	30 "	7½ "	950.00	2500.00
Single	30 "	5 "	33 "	8 "	1000.00	3000.00

THE WITTEMANN BI-PLANE GLIDER

No. 12

Greatest Lifting Power per square foot of surface. Strongest and Lightest construction of select spruce, varnished. Weight 54 lbs., carrying 200 lbs. and over.

Taking Down and Setting Up.—The main frame is detachable by joints in the center. The uprights are inserted in sockets. The wire braces are already attached, being firmly fastened at one end and loosely at the other to allow for spanning after framework has been set up.

Shipping.—Folded and packed in crate about 11 feet by 5 feet by 1 foot. Every precaution is taken to reduce size and weight of crate to make carriage expenses as low as possible for the purchaser.

Price, including crating and delivery f. o. b. cars New York City, **$75.00.**

The above Glider always carried in stock. Other sizes made to order.

INSTRUCTIONS FOR SETTING UP AND OPERATING THE WITTEMANN GLIDER No. 12.

TOOLS—A screw driver and pair of flat nosed pliers.

MAIN FRAME—After removing sections of planes from crate insert the uprights into the sockets, taking care to put the beveled edge to conform with the castings, then tighten up on the thumb-nuts. Do not put any unnecessary strain on these, it being sufficient to tighten with fingers only. After having done this you will have two rigid frames. Proceed to slip together at corresponding joints and tighten bolts.

TAIL—Slip the two wings in place where bolt holes are provided for, insert bolts and tighten, which will leave the tail complete. Then insert the two ends in sockets on the main frame; push the two split pins in the holes provided for same, bending the ends slightly to keep from working out, then cross the cords on each side, snap these in place on eye-bolt at second uprights from end of frame.

To take a glide, grip under your arm-pits the parallel bars of the lower plane, and run with it against the wind, keeping the machine fairly level, so as to encounter least resistance. When speed is obtained, tilt the planes slightly upwards, and you will be lifted off your feet. Begin with making short jumps, gradually take longer ones, and then soar.

For lateral balance on glider, when in flight, throw your legs over to the high side. This will put the machine on an even keel. Try to have the machine glide with planes tilted slightly upwards. In descending, tilt more, so as to offer resistance to the wind and to land easily. Make all movements gradually avoiding excess, and you will enjoy the sport.

In winds from 15 to 30 miles per hour you can start on level ground by attaching a good quality of sash cord to each end of forward part of lower plane. See that it is securely tied to the main stick. The cord need not be longer than ten feet. Then let an assistant at each end let out about five feet of cord for the start, they running a little to start you in a calm. When the wind is strong enough you will go straight up in the air, after tilting machine slightly upwards in front to catch the wind. Then your assistants may run with you in your practice flight till you have obtained confidence in machine. A half dozen trials will convince you of the fun that can be obtained and show you the practical way of handling the machine.

Beginners should not attempt to glide in winds over 20 miles per hour.

121

LAMINATED RIBS.

The functions of the ribs herein described will be found satisfactory for all ordinary conditions. The requirements of special ribs vary greatly and occasionally have to be especially designed to meet certain conditions. We are prepared to supply such ribs and solicit inquiries, which should be accompanied by plans, together with a description of what is desired to be accomplished.

Our improved methods insure accuracy in manufacture as all our ribs are made from well-seasoned spruce, straight grained and free from knots, wind shakes, &c. They are shaped and dressed, fitted with sockets (same as Figures 1 F, 2 F, 3 F, 4 F, 5 F, specified on page 12); also bored for fastening to main beams, besides having holes for lacing the cloth thereon.

When ordering specify type and size of rib wanted.

Single Cover Type.

Length	Type	Material	Price
4 Ft. 6 In.	Heavy No. 1, 3, 5, 8	Spruce	$1.72
5 " "	"	"	1.93
5 " 6 "	"	"	2.15
6 " "	"	"	2.36
6 " 6 "	"	"	2.57
4 " "	Medium No. 2, 6	"	1.29
5 " "	"	"	1.43
5 " 6 "	"	"	1.57
6 " "	"	"	1.72
6 " 6 "	"	"	1.86
4 " "	Light No. 4, 7, 9	"	.86
5 " "	"	"	1.00
5 " 6 "	"	"	1.14
6 " "	"	"	1.29
6 " 6 "	"	"	1.43

Double Cover Type.

Length	Type	Style	Material	Price
4 Ft. 6 in.	Heavy No. 10		Spruce	$2.86
5 " "	"		"	3.15
5 " 6 "	"		"	3.43
6 " "	"		"	3.79
6 " 6 "	"		"	4.15
4 " "	Light No. 11		"	2.74
5 " "	"		"	3.00
5 " 6 "	"		"	3.29
6 " "	"		"	3.65
6 " 6 "	"		"	4.00

Block Ribs.

Length	Type	Material	Price
5 "	Regular No. 12	"	1.14
6 "	"	"	1.36
7 "	"	"	1.57
8 "	"	"	1.86

Channel Ribs.

Length	Type	Style	Material	Price
5 "	Heavy No. 14		"	2.15
6 "	"		"	2.57
7 "	"		"	3.00
8 "	"		"	3.43
5 "	Light		"	1.43
6 "	"		"	1.72
7 "	"		"	2.00
8 "	"		"	2.29

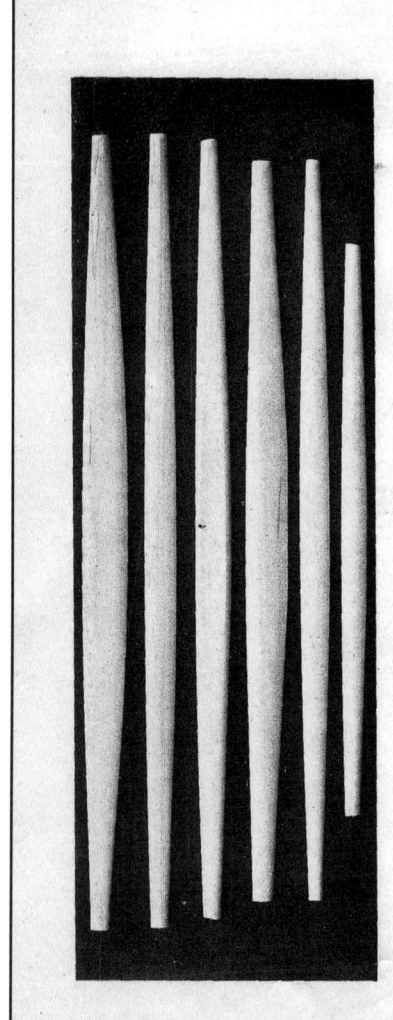

VERTICAL STRUTS

Our vertical struts are made of spruce, selected for stiffness, uniformly-shaped, and offering the least head resistance to the air. Shaped at ends to fit our standard sockets.

Length	Type	Style	Material	Price
4 Ft. 6 In.	Heavy	Fish shaped	Spruce	$1.36
5 " 6 "	"	"	"	1.57
5 " 6 "	"	"	"	1.72
6 " 6 "	"	"	"	2.00
6 " 6 "	"	"	"	2.22
4 " 6 "	Medium	"	"	1.22
5 " 6 "	"	"	"	1.36
5 " 6 "	"	"	"	1.50
6 " 6 "	"	"	"	1.72

Length	Type	Style	Material	Price
6 " 6 "	Medium	Fish shaped	Spruce	$1.86
4 " 6 "	Light	"	"	1.14
5 " 6 "	"	"	"	1.29
5 " 6 "	"	"	"	1.43
6 " 6 "	"	"	"	1.57
6 " 6 "	"	"	"	1.72

When ordering vertical struts state what size and type of sockets are to be used.

LIST OF FINISHED SPRUCE.

PRICE PER FOOT.

Size in.	$\frac{1}{4}$	$\frac{3}{8}$	$\frac{1}{2}$	$\frac{5}{8}$	$\frac{3}{4}$	$\frac{7}{8}$	1	$1\frac{1}{8}$	$1\frac{1}{4}$	$1\frac{3}{8}$	$1\frac{1}{2}$	$1\frac{5}{8}$	$1\frac{3}{4}$	$1\frac{7}{8}$	2
$\frac{1}{4}$	.03														
$\frac{3}{8}$	.04	.04													
$\frac{1}{2}$	.04	.04	.06												
$\frac{5}{8}$	.06	.06	.06	.06											
$\frac{3}{4}$	.06	.07	.06	.06	.06										
$\frac{7}{8}$	.06	.07	.06	.06	.06	.06									
1	.07	.07	.06	.06	.06	.06	.07								
$1\frac{1}{8}$		.07	.07	.07	.07	.07	.07	.07							
$1\frac{1}{4}$			.07	.07	.07	.07	.07	.07	.09						
$1\frac{3}{8}$			.07	.07	.07	.09	.09	.09	.09	.10					
$1\frac{1}{2}$			.07	.07	.07	.09	.09	.09	.10	.10	.11				
$1\frac{5}{8}$			.07	.09	.09	.09	.09	.10	.10	.11	.11	.13			
$1\frac{3}{4}$			.09	.09	.09	.10	.10	.10	.11	.11	.13	.13	.14		
$1\frac{7}{8}$			.09	.09	.09	.10	.10	.11	.11	.13	.13	.14	.14	.16	
2			.10	.10	.10	.11	.11	.11	.13	.13	.14	.14	.16	.16	.17
$2\frac{1}{8}$				.10	.10	.11	.11	.13	.13	.14	.14	.16	.16	.17	.17
$2\frac{1}{4}$				.11	.11	.13	.13	.13	.14	.14	.16	.16	.17	.17	.19
$2\frac{3}{8}$				.11	.11	.13	.13	.14	.14	.16	.16	.17	.17	.19	.19
$2\frac{1}{2}$					.13	.14	.14	.14	.16	.16	.17	.17	.19	.19	.20
$2\frac{5}{8}$					.13	.14	.14	.16	.16	.17	.17	.19	.19	.20	.20
$2\frac{3}{4}$					.14	.16	.16	.16	.17	.17	.19	.19	.20	.20	.21
$2\frac{7}{8}$					.14	.16	.16	.17	.17	.19	.19	.20	.20	.21	.23
3					.16	.17	.17	.17	.19	.19	.20	.20	.21	.21	.23

This spruce is specially selected for Aeroplane Construction, free from knots and other imperfections. Lengths over 10 feet add 25% to list.

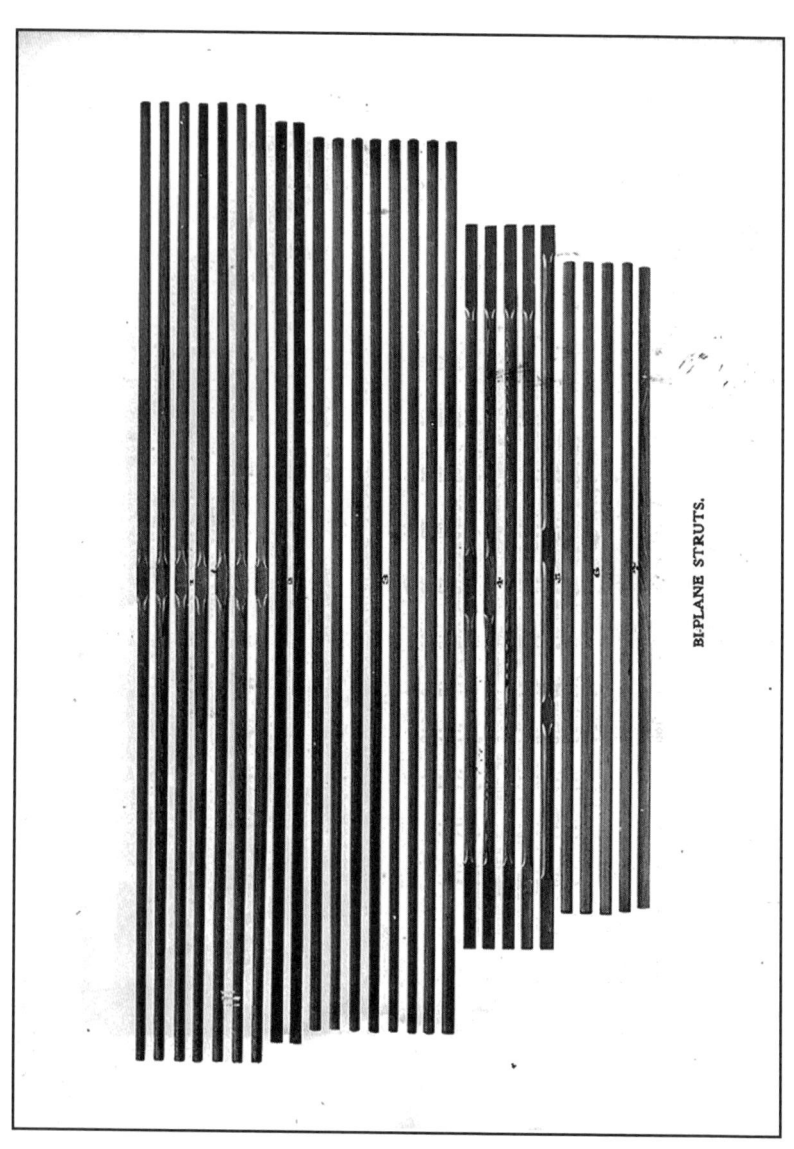
BI-PLANE STRUTS.

BIPLANE STRUTS

Our Bi-plane Struts are made of spruce, selected for stiffness, shaped uniformly, and fit our standard size couplings. They are supplied in various lengths, sizes and shapes. Those shown in cut are for standard planes.

No. 1 Outriggers for Front or Rear Control of Biplane

Size	Tapered	Material	Description	Price per ft.
1 1/16 x 1 7/8 in.	1 7/8 x 1 3/8 in.	Spruce	Fish shape	.23c
1 3/8 x 2 in.	"	"	"	.26c

No. 2 Braces

| 1 in. x 1 3/4 in. | Ash | .17c |
| 1 3/8 x 2 in. | " | .20c |

No. 3 and 6 Main Lateral Beams

| 1 1/8 in. x 1 5/8 in. | Spruce | Oval | .16c |
| 1 3/8 in. x 1 3/4 in. | " | " | .17c |

No. 4 Lateral Braces

| 1 in. x 1 1/2 in. | Fish shaped | .16c |
| 1 1/16 in. x 1 5/8 in. | " | .17c |

No. 5 Main Skids

| 1 3/4 in. x 2 in. | .40c |
| 2 in. x 2 1/4 in. | .43c |

No. 7 Main Lateral Beam Supports

| 1 1/16 in. x 1 5/8 in. | Ash | Concave | .20c |
| 1 3/8 in. x 1 3/4 in. | " | " | .23c |

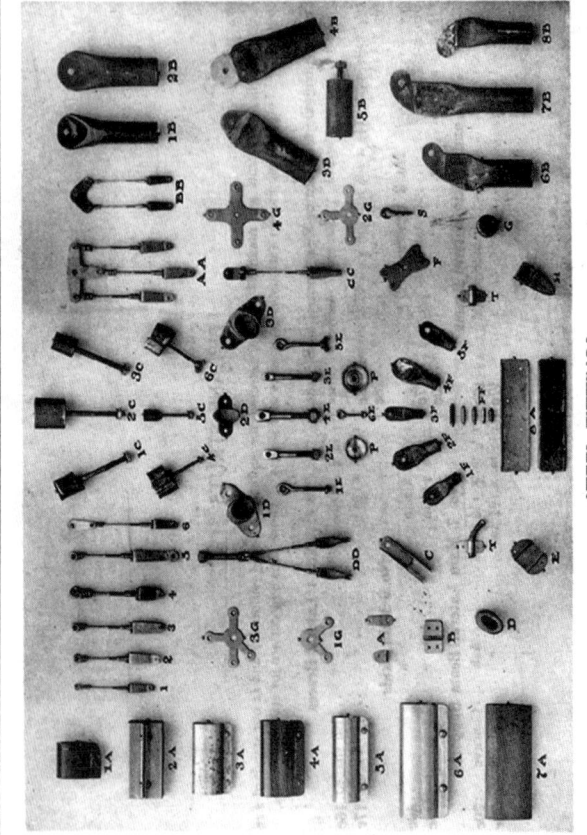

STEEL FITTINGS

The Steel Fittings shown in these pages will be found appropriate for building aeroplanes of various classes. Attention is directed to the large assortment of sizes that are listed, which cover, we believe, every condition and requirement.

These sizes offer a wide range of choice, and ordering other sizes should be avoided as much as possible, inasmuch as special patterns necessary in manufacture involves additional expense and also causes the usual delay in executing orders for special goods. When ordering fittings, specify number and size of article with which same are to be used.

STEEL FITTINGS

Couplings.

No.	Inside measure	Length	Type	Price
1—A	1 1-16 in. x 1⅝ in.	1⅞ in.	Oval	50c
	1⅛ in. x 1¾ in	in. “	“	50c
	1⅛ in. x 2 in	“	“	57c
2—A	1 1-16 in. x 1⅝ in	4 in	Oblong	57c
	1⅛ in. x 1⅜ in	“	“	57c
	1⅛ in. x 2 in.	“	“	72c
3—A 4—A	1 1-16 in. x 1⅝ in	3 or 4 in.	Oval	57c
	1 1-8 in. x 1⅜ in	“	“	57c
	1 1-8 in. x 2 in	“	“	72c
5—A	1 in	4 in.	Round	43c
	1 1-8 in	4½ in.	“	43c
	1¼ in	5 in.	“	50c
6—A	1 1-8 in. x 1⅞ in	6 in.	Oval	72c
	1 1-8 in. x 2 in	“	“	72c
	1¼ in. x 2¼ in	“	“	79c
7—A	1 1-16 in. x 1⅝ in	4 in.	“	72c
	1⅛ in. x 2 in	5 in.	Made of	79c
	1 1-8 in. 2½ in	6 in.	Seamless tub'g	86c
8—A	1½ in	6 in.	Flanged	72c
	1¾ in	“	“	79c

Vertical Sockets.

No.	Inside measure	Length	Type	Price
1—C	1 in	4½ in.	Round bevel	43c
	1 1-16 in	“	“	43c
	1 1-8 in.	“	“	50c
2—C	1 in. x 1⅝ in	5 in.	Oval	72c
	1 1-16 in. x 1⅝ in	“	“	72c
	1 1-8 in. x 1¾ in	“	“	79c

No.	Inside measure	Length	Type	Price
3—C	1 in	4½ in.	Round	43c
	1 1-16 in	“	“	43c
	1 1-8 in	“	“	50c
4—C 6—C	½ in. x 1¼ in	3 in.	Oval	43c
	5-8 in. x 1¼ in	“	“	43c
	¾ in. x 1½ in	“	“	50c
5—C	½ in	3 in.	Round	29c
	⅝ in	“	“	29c
	¾ in	“	“	36c
1—D	⅞ in. x 1¼ in	1 1-2 in.	All	36c
2—D	1 1-16 in. x 1 7-16 in	“	Standard sizes	43c
3—D	1 1-8 in. x 1½ in	1⅝ in	in Stock	43c

Outrigger Sockets.

No.	Inside measure	Length	Type	Price
1—B 2—B	1 in. x 1 1-4 in	5½ in.	Oval	64c
	1 1-16 in. x 1 3-8 in	“	or	64c
	1 1-8 in. x 1½ in.	“	Round	72c
3—B 4—B	1 in. x 1 1-4 in	6 in.	Oval	$1.07
	1 1-16 in. x 1 3-8 in.	“	or	1.07
	1 1-8 in. x 1 1-2 in.	“	Round	1.14
5—B	1 in. x 1 1-4 in	3 in.	Oval	72c
	1 1-16 in. x 1 3-8 in	“	or	72c
	1 1-8 in. x 1 1-2 in.	“	Round	79c
6—B 7—B 8—B	1 in. x 1 1-4 in	6 in.	Oval	$1.14
	1 1-16 in. x 1⅜ in.	“	or	1.14
	1 1-8 in. x 1 1-2 in.	“	Round	1.22

STEEL FITTINGS—Continued.

Rib Sockets

No.	Inside measure	Length	Type	Price
1—F, 2—F	$\frac{7}{16}$ in.	2⅜	Round	14c
3—F, 4—F	$\frac{9}{16}$ in.	2¾	"	17c
5—F	$\frac{11}{16}$ in.	"	"	20c

Turnbuckles

No.	Breaking strength approximate	Type	Price
1	300lbs.	Standard	19c
2	500 "	"	24c
3	600 "	Riveted head	29c
4	1000 "	"	43c
5	500 "	with ex. long head	29c
6	500 "	" rear connection	31c

Turnbuckles with Connections

No.	Type of connection	Price
AA	3—Way Spider with No. 2 turnbuckle	87c
BB	2— " " " " " "	63c
CC	1— " " " " " "	33c
DD	2E—Eyebolt with No. 1 turnbuckle	47c
DD	3E— " " " 2 "	57c
DD	4E— " " " 3 "	64c

Eyebolts

No.	Dia.	Length	Price
1—E	$\frac{3}{16}$ in.	2 in.	14c
2—E	¼ "	2¼ "	29c
3—E	$\frac{5}{16}$ "	2¼ "	31c
4—E	⅜ "	2½ "	36c
5—E	$\frac{3}{16}$ "	2½ "	17c

Spiders

No.	No. of legs	Price
1—G	2	14c
2—G	3	14c
3—G	4	14c
4—G	4	14c

Seamless Ferrules

No.	Length	Dia.	Hole	Steel (Per 100)	Brass (Per 100)
FF	$\frac{5}{8}$ in.	$\frac{3}{16}$ in.	$\frac{1}{8}$ in.	$5.72	$4.29
	$\frac{3}{4}$ in.	$\frac{1}{4}$ "	$\frac{3}{16}$ "	6.44	5.01
	$\frac{7}{8}$ "	$\frac{1}{4}$ "	$\frac{3}{16}$ "	6.79	6.08

Steel Fittings

No.	Size	Description	price
A	$\frac{3}{4}$ in. x $\frac{7}{8}$ in.	Corner brace	09c
B	1 in. x 2 in.	Clamp hinge	36c
C	$\frac{3}{4}$ in. x $3\frac{1}{4}$ in.	Clamp hinge bottom pivot	36c
D	1 in. x $1\frac{1}{2}$ in.	Sleeves to protect end of struts	29c
E	$\frac{7}{8}$ in. x $\frac{7}{8}$ in.	Sliding clamp	14c
F	$1\frac{3}{8}$ in. x $2\frac{3}{4}$ in.	Rudder hinge support	21c
G	1 in.	Sleeves to protect end of struts	29c
H	$\frac{7}{8}$ in. x $\frac{7}{8}$ in. to $\frac{3}{4}$ in.	Reducing strut connection	43c
P-P	$1\frac{1}{2}$ in.	Pulley wheels for cable transmission	36c
S	$1\frac{3}{4}$ in.	Snap hooks	14c
T-T	$\frac{3}{8}$ in.	Steering cable supports (Copper)	36c
	$1\frac{1}{2}$ in.	Side pulleys made especially for steering cable	1.43
	$\frac{5}{8}$ in. x $\frac{3}{4}$ in.	U shapped light rib clamp	07c

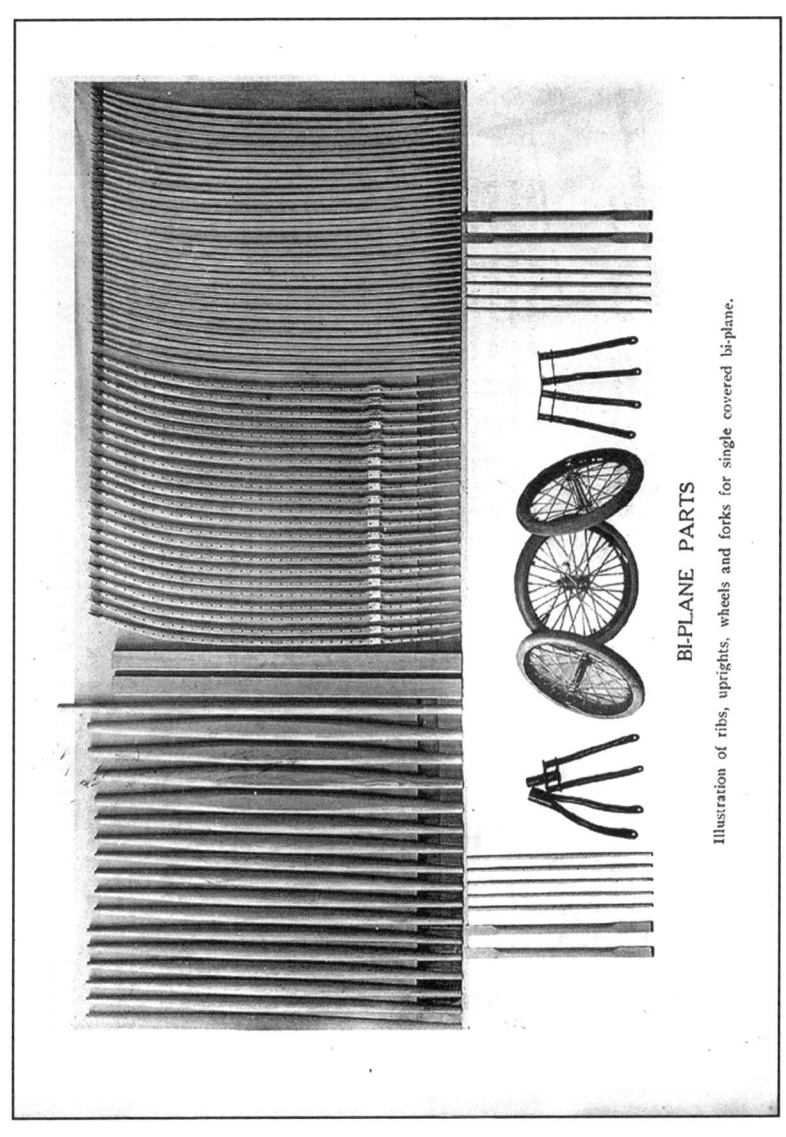

BI-PLANE PARTS

Illustration of ribs, uprights, wheels and forks for single covered bi-plane.

CONTROLS.

No. 1 Front or Rear Elevator

Length	Width	Material	Price Skeleton	Price Covered Naid No. 6 A
7 ft.	2 ft. 4 in.	spruce	$15.00	$28.50
8 "	2 " 8 "	"	17.25	31.50
9 "	3 "	"	19.25	34.25

No. 2 Ailerons

7 ft.	2 ft. 4 in.	spruce	$12.50	$25.75
8 "	2 " 8 "	"	14.25	28.50
9 "	3 "	"	16.00	31.50

No. 3 Box Elevator Type —Each Plane—

Length	Width	Material	Price Skeleton	Price Covered Naid No. 6 A
7 ft.	2 ft. 4 in.	spruce	$11.00	$24.25
8 "	2 " 8 "	"	12.50	26.50
9 "	3 "	"	14.00	28.50

No. 4 Vertical Rudder

3 ft.	2 ft. 6 in.	spruce	$ 8.50	$15.75
3 "	6 in. 2 " 6 "	"	10.75	18.00
4 "	3 " 6 "	"	11.50	19.50

CLOTH.

Goodyear Rubber Coated Aeroplane Fabrics

Rubber coated Fabrics have distinct advantages for Aeroplane construction. The rubber coating makes the fabric air proof and preserves it from atmospheric action. Also this coating prevents absorption of moisture. This keeps the fabric light in weight under all conditions—a point of great importance.

Cloth No.	Weight per sq. yd.	Strength per inch warp	weft	width	Price per yd.
6	4¾ oz.	80 lbs.	65 lbs.	36 in.	$1.50
7	4½ "	80 "	75 "	36 "	1.40
8	4½ "	60 "	55 "	40 "	1.00
10	6½ "	100 "	90 "	40 "	1.25

Naiad Aeronautical Cloth

No.	Width	Break at lbs. per in.	Tears at lbs.	Weight per sq. yd.	Price per yd.
1	36 in.	25	1	3.26 oz.	$ .32
2	38 "	57	2	5.50 "	.60
6 A	35 "	70	10	5.8 "	.75
7	36 "	32	1¼	2.25 "	1.25
35	36 "	45	2	.5	.48

First—Elasticity with the least amount of stretch, lightness and strength.

Second—To protect the cloth from moisture by applying a moisture proof coating, making it airtight and leaving it with a smooth non-resisting surface, and preventing expansion or contraction from moisture or heat. The coating is sufficiently elastic to withstand any stretch in the cloth and will also stand any amount of cold or heat, remaining unchanged under these extremes, and showing no tendency to become either hard or sticky.

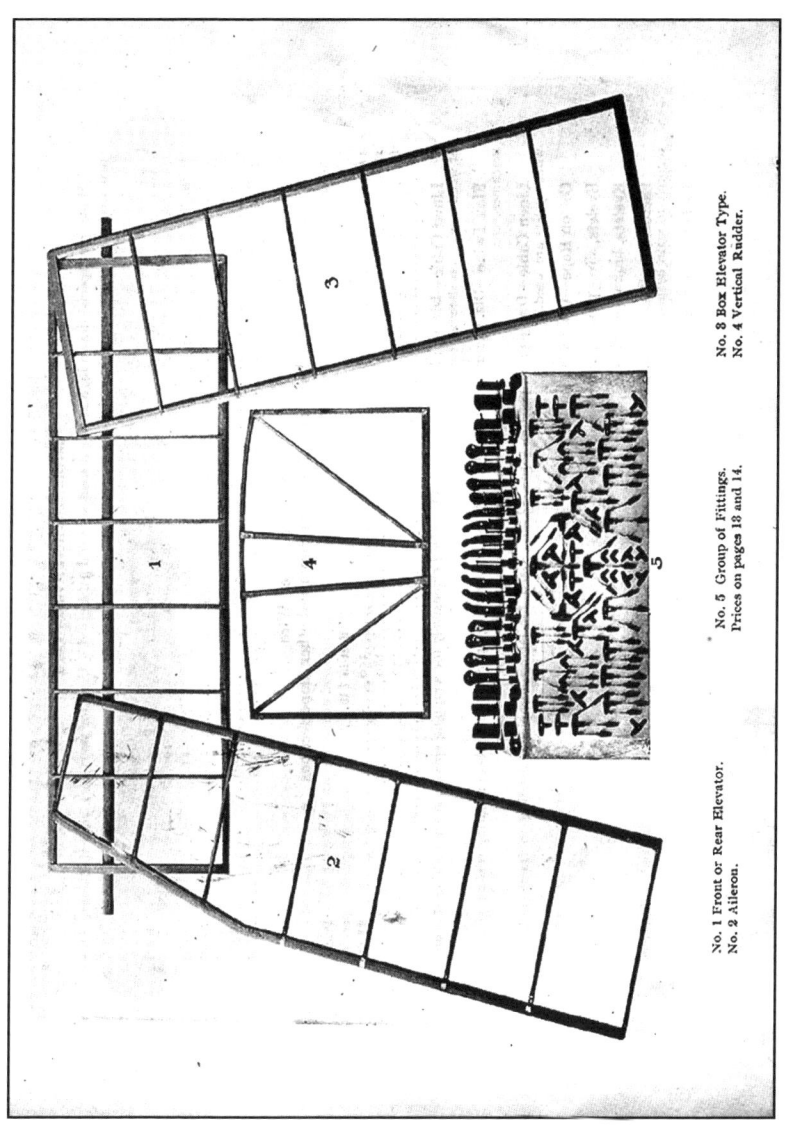

No. 1 Front or Rear Elevator.
No. 2 Aileron.

No. 3 Box Elevator Type.
No. 4 Vertical Rudder.

No. 5 Group of Fittings.
Prices on pages 13 and 14.

Galvanized Steel Aviator Cord

Made from special drawn high strength steel wire and galvanized. Used for stays on Flying Machines. Has great strength, is light in weight and flexible.

Dia.	No. of Wires	Approximate Breaking Strength in pounds	Weight in Pounds per 100 ft.	Price Per Ft.
1/8 in.	19	2,300	3.60	.04½c
3/16 "	"	1,465	2.80	.03½c
1/4 "	"	800	2.	.03 c
3/32 "	"	500	.96	.02½c
1/16 "	"	200	.35	.02 c
3/32 "	7			

Imported Steel Wire
The Best Made, Free from Flaws and other Imperfections

No.	Dia.	Feet in 1 lb.	Price per lb.
14	.032	350	$1.00
16	.036	280	"
18	.04	230	"
20	.044	180	"

Linen Cable—Dia. 1-32 in., per 1-2 lb. **$1.00.** Used extensively for wrapping splices, strengthening sections of wood sewing on sheeting to frame, etc.

Flax Twine—Dia. 1-32 in., per 1-2 lb. **95c.** Used for wrapping splices and bamboo, securing ribs on gliding machines, etc.

Linen Cable—Dia. 3-32 in., per 100 yards, **$2.00.** Used for lacing aeroplane sheeting to frame and ribs when eyelets are used.

Cotton Rope—Dia. 1-8 in., per lb, **70c.**

Eyelets, silver plated, per thousand, **50c.**

Eyelets, brown, per thousand, **50c.**

Escutcheon Pins per lb, **75c.** When eyelets are used with sheeting, same may be fastened with these securely to main beams.

Tools for fastening eyelets, **$1.75.**

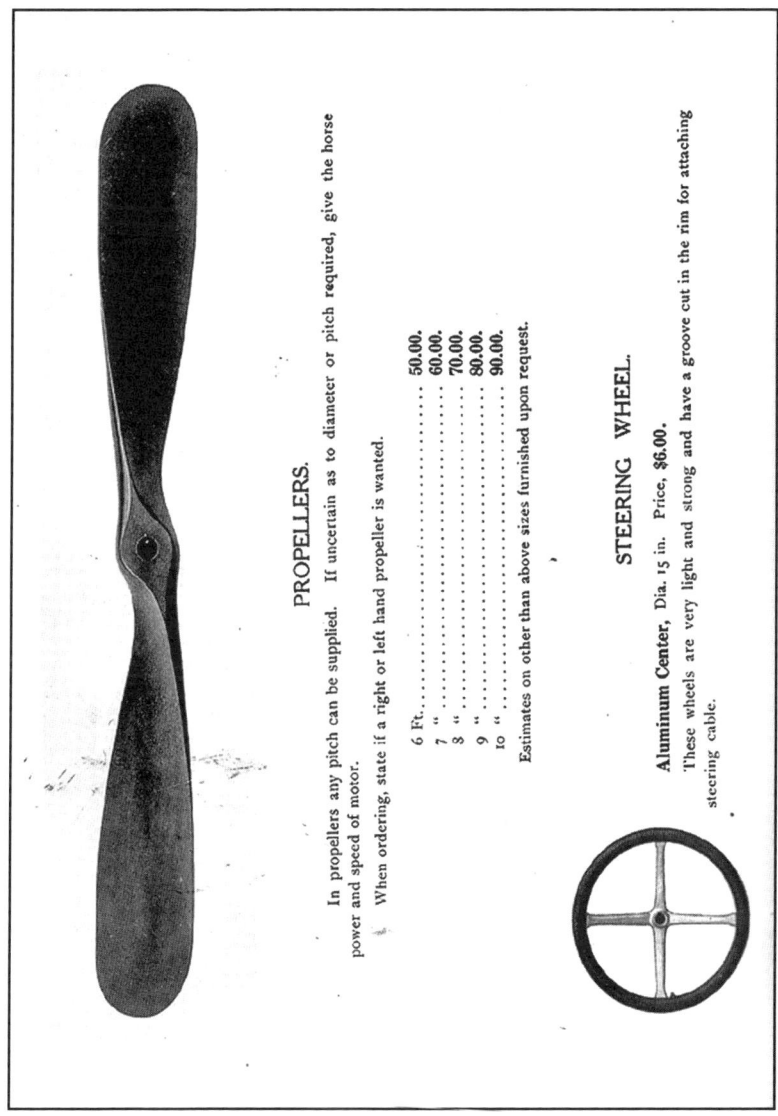

PROPELLERS.

In propellers any pitch can be supplied. If uncertain as to diameter or pitch required, give the horse power and speed of motor.

When ordering, state if a right or left hand propeller is wanted.

6 Ft............ **50.00.**
7 " .... **60.00.**
8 " .... **70.00.**
9 " .... **80.00.**
10 " .... **90.00.**

Estimates on other than above sizes furnished upon request.

STEERING WHEEL.

Aluminum Center, Dia. 15 in. Price, **$6.00.**

These wheels are very light and strong and have a groove cut in the rim for attaching steering cable.

RADIATORS—LIGHT WEIGHT

H. P.	Width	Height	Weight	Type	Price
35	14 in.	19 in.	32 lbs.	Honey Comb	$45.00
45	15 "	20 "	34 "	"	55.00
60	16 "	22 "	37 "	"	70.00
90	25 "	24 "	52 "	"	85.00

FEATHER WEIGHT

35	14 in.	19 in.	24 lbs.	Honey Comb	$45.00
45	15 "	20 "	26 "	"	55.00
60	16 "	22 "	30 "	"	70.00
90	27 "	24 "	40 "	"	85.00

GASOLENE TANKS—COPPER

Gallons	Dia.	Length	Weight	Type	Price
1½	5 in.	24 in.	2½ lbs.	Torpedo Head	$ 5.25
2	6 "	25 "	3 "	"	6.50
3	6½ "	31 "	3¾ "	"	7.25
5	7½ "	36 "	5¼ "	"	8.00
7½	9 "	39 "	6½ "	"	10.50
10	10 "	45 "	7¾ "	"	12.00
15	12 "	47 "	9½ "	"	17.00
20	13 "	52 "	11 "	"	21.00

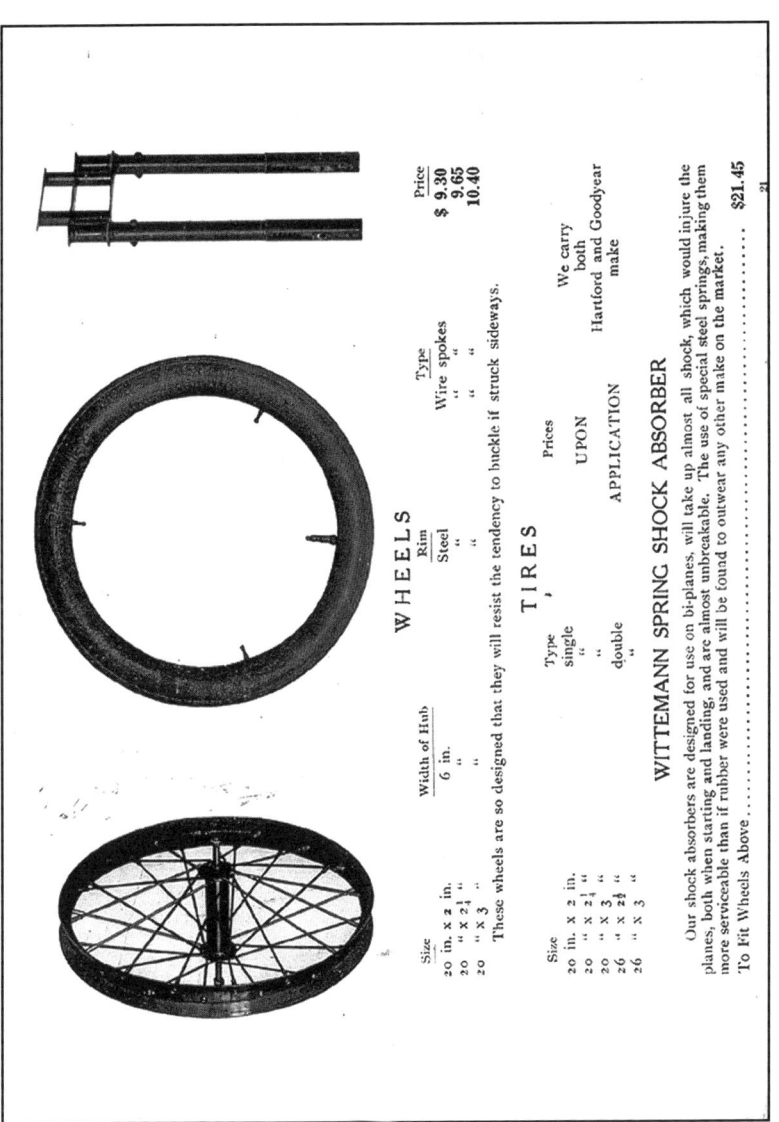

WHEELS

Size	Width of Hub	Rim	Type	Price
20 in. x 2 in.	6 in.	Steel	Wire spokes	$ 9.30
20 " x 2¼ "	"	"	"	9.65
20 " x 3 "	"	"	"	10.40

These wheels are so designed that they will resist the tendency to buckle if struck sideways.

TIRES

Size	Type	Prices
20 in. x 2 in.	single	UPON
20 " x 2¼ "	"	
20 " x 3 "	"	APPLICATION
26 " x 2½ "	double	We carry both
26 " x 3 "	"	Hartford and Goodyear make

WITTEMANN SPRING SHOCK ABSORBER

Our shock absorbers are designed for use on bi-planes, will take up almost all shock, which would injure the planes, both when starting and landing, and are almost unbreakable. The use of special steel springs, making them more serviceable than if rubber were used and will be found to outwear any other make on the market.
To Fit Wheels Above.. $21.45

ROUND COLD DRAWN STEEL TUBING

Prices Per Foot—Outside Diameter

		1-4 in.	3-8 in.	1-2 in.	3-4 in.	1 in.	1 1-4 in.	1 1-2 in.	2 in.
B. W. Gauge	22	.15	.15	.15	.19	.21	.23	.26	..
	20	.15	.15	.15	.19	.21	.23	.26	.52
	18	.16	.16	.16	.20	.23	.26	.30	.52
	16	.18	.18	.18	.22	.25	.30	.35	.52

These sizes are furnished in three different tempers—hard, medium and soft.

The hard temper is used where great rigidity and stiffness are required, and where tubes are not to be bent or manipulated in any way that would change their form.

The medium temper is used where strength and toughness are required, and where only a slight or medium change of form is wanted.

The soft temper is used where the tubes must be manipulated and where a decided change of form is required that demands ductile and pliable material.

BALL BEARINGS

Especially adapted for both thrust and radial bearing of propellor shaft. These bearings are enclosed in a casing and are all assembled ready to be slipped into place.

RADIAL CONE BEARINGS.

Shaft Diam.	Outside Diam.	Width.	Balls.	List Price
1¼ in.	3¼ in.	¾ in.	⅜ in.	$ 7.00
1½ in.	3½ in.	¾ in.	⅜ in.	10.00
1¾ in.	4⅜ in.	1 in.	½ in.	18.00

RADIAL RING BEARINGS.

Bore inches	Diam. inches	Width inches	Load in lbs.	List Price
1.5748	3.1496	0.7086	860	$7.25
1.7716	3.3464	0.7480	950	8.50
1.9685	3.5433	0.7874	1000	10.00
2.1653	3.9370	0.8268	1160	12.00

A SECTION OF OUR FACTORY, SHOWING ASSEMBLING DIVISION.

Photo Credits

The Author would like to acknowledge the following individuals and organizations for supplying photos, postcards, etc. from their collections. This book would be much less interesting without their contributions.

Page 7: *The Richmond County Democrat* (December 12, 1896)
Page 8: Ed Bruder
Page 9: (Top) Ed Bruder
       (Bottom) Mark Nathans
Page 11: Aviation Hall of Fame & Museum of New Jersey
Page 12: (Both) Aviation Hall of Fame & Museum of New Jersey
Page 13: (Both) Aviation Hall of Fame & Museum of New Jersey
Page 14: Aviation Hall of Fame & Museum of New Jersey
Page 15: Ed Bruder
Page 16: (Top) Smithsonian National Air & Space Museum
       (Bottom) Mark Nathans
Page 17: Ed Drury
Page 18: Ed Drury
Page 20: *Aviation* Magazine, 1916
Page 21: *Aviation* Magazine, 1917
Page 24: Ed Drury
Page 25: Ed Drury
Page 26: (Top) Ed Bruder
       (Bottom) Gary Williams
Page 27: Aviation Hall of Fame & Museum of New Jersey
Page 28: (Top) Louis Judice
       (Bottom) Jessica Kratz
Page 30: Ed Drury
Page 31: Ed Bruder
Page 33: Ed Drury
Page 34: (Both) Ed Bruder
Page 35: Ed Drury
Page 36: Steve Remington
Page 37: (Both) Louis Judice
Page 38: (Both) Louis Judice
Page 39: (Both) Louis Judice

Page 41: Ted Lovington
Page 42: (Both) Ted Lovington
Page 43: (Both) Ted Lovington
Page 44: (Top) Ted Lovington
(Bottom, Left & Right) Ed Drury
Page 45: Albert Davis
Page 46: Albert Davis
Page 47: Albert Davis
Page 48: Albert Davis
Page 49: Ed Drury
Page 50: (Both) Ed Drury
Page 51: (Top) Gateway National Recreation Area
(Bottom) Ed Drury
Page 52: (Top) Gateway National Recreation Area
(Bottom) Ed Bruder
Page 53: (Top) Gateway National Recreation Area
(Bottom) Ed Bruder
Page 54: Ed Bruder
Page 55: (Top) Ed Drury
(Bottom) Rick Thompson
Page 56: Ed Drury
Page 57: *Time* Magazine
Page 58: Aerofiles.com
Page 59: Ed Bruder
Page 60: Koble Collection via Dover Litho
Page 62: Dan Cullman
Page 63: (Both) Dan Cullman
Page 65: Ed Drury
Page 66: Malcolm Boreham
Page 67: (Both) Walter Boyne
Page 68: Walter Boyne
Page 69: Walter Boyne
Page 70: Ed Drury
Page 71: Unknown Aviation Magazine
Page 73: Ed Drury
Page 74: (Top) John Schultz
(Bottom) Ed Drury
Page 75: Aerofiles.com
Page 76: (Both) August Tornquist

Page 77: (Both) August Tornquist

Page 78: (Top) August Tornquist
         (Bottom) Jeffery Guido
Page 79: (Top) August Tornquist
         (Bottom) Jim Stamper
Page 80: Ed Drury
Page 81: Ed Drury
Page 83: (Top) Ed Bruder
         (Bottom) Ed Drury
Page 84: Jim Stamper
Page 85: (Top) Ed Drury
         (Bottom) Kari Dienstadt
Page 86: (Top) Andy Origlia
         (Bottom) Ed Drury
Page 87: (Top) Ed Drury
         (Center) Andy Origlia
         (Bottom) Charles Modzelewski
Page 88: (Top) Jeffery Guido
         (Center) Andy Origlia
         (Bottom) Charles Modzelewski
Page 89: Andy Origlia
Page 90: (Top) Ed Drury
         (Bottom) Ed Fanuzzi
Page 91: (Top) Ed Fanuzzi
         (Center) Charles Modzelewski
         (Bottom) Ed Fanuzzi
Page 92: August Tornquist
Appendix: Ed Drury